IN THE **TIME** OF

The Atlanta Braves, Their Manager,

BOBBY COX

My Couch, Two Decades, and Me

Lang Whitaker

SCRIBNER

New York   London   Toronto   Sydney

SCRIBNER
A Division of Simon & Schuster, Inc.
1230 Avenue of the Americas
New York, NY 10020

First Scribner hardcover edition March 2011

SCRIBNER and design are registered trademarks of The Gale Group, Inc.,
used under license by Simon & Schuster, Inc., the publisher of this work.

For information about special discounts for bulk purchases,
please contact Simon & Schuster Special Sales at 1-866-506-1949
or business@simonandschuster.com.

The Simon & Schuster Speakers Bureau can bring authors to your live event.
For more information or to book an event contact the Simon & Schuster Speakers
Bureau at 1-866-248-3049 or visit our website at www.simonspeakers.com.

Designed by Carla Jayne Jones

Manufactured in the United States of America

1   3   5   7   9   10   8   6   4   2

Library of Congress Cataloging-in-Publication Data

Whitaker, Lang.
In the time of Bobby Cox : the Atlanta Braves, their manager, my couch, two decades, and
me / Lang Whitaker.—1st Scribner hardcover ed.
        p.   cm.
1. Atlanta Braves (Baseball team). 2. Cox, Bobby, 1941–. 3. Baseball managers—
United States. 4. Whitaker, Lang. I. Title.
GV875.A8W48 2011
796.357'6409758231—dc22   2010036177

ISBN 978-1-4391-4838-9
ISBN 978-1-4391-5263-8 (ebook)

For Isabel

CONTENTS

Contents

IN THE **TIME** OF **BOBBY COX**

INTRODUCTION
Sundays with Bobby

I'm worried. I'm really, really worried. It is a balmy Wednesday night toward the end of July 2007. My wife is asleep. I am with my dog, Starbury, in my apartment on the Upper West Side of Manhattan. The window is open, but the curtains are drawn; the apartment is dark, and I am sitting on the left side of the couch, same spot as always, my bare feet resting on the IKEA coffee table with the gently warped top exactly where my wife doesn't like me to rest my feet because it's also where we place our dinner plates.

The Atlanta Braves are on my TV. The Braves are almost always on my TV. If I'm home during the baseball season, I'm watching the Braves play. If I'm not home when they're playing, I'm recording the game so I can watch it later.

I especially love it when the Braves go out West. The games start late at night, East Coast time. I can put my wife to bed, then crash out on the couch and watch until the wee hours of the night. Tonight, for instance, the Braves are playing the Giants out in San Fran at whatever the current name of their park is, the one with the bay beyond right field. First pitch is around 10:05 p.m. in New York, which means the game won't end until close to 1:00 a.m. Tonight's game has a nominal national relevance, because Barry Bonds is only three home runs away from breaking Hank Aaron's all-time career record, though I'm past caring about that, and so, seemingly, is the rest of the country. I guess one of the side effects of the steroid era is public ambivalence. What matters to me tonight is that the Braves are 3 games back of the New York Mets with about 50 games left to play. And, like I said, I'm worried. I'm really, really worried.

Our first basemen have combined to post the worst batting average at any position in the major leagues. Will Jarrod Saltalamacchia or Brian McCann get the start behind the plate tonight? Has McCann's left ring finger healed completely? Willie Harris is no Willie Mays, but he's still been slumping lately; we need him to get going again. We should trade Salty, right? Andruw Jones is down to about one home run a week and is again starting to lose his balance at the plate. Has hitting coach Terry Pendleton noticed this yet? If not, why not? It's taken nearly two decades, but I've finally started to come around on Chipper Jones; the guy can flat-out hit. The back end of our rotation is beginning to stabilize, and lefty rookie Jo-Jo Reyes has me intrigued. The bullpen, though, is a disaster; I hate to say that it reminds me a little bit of last season's pen, but they're heading in that direction. Something's wrong with reliever Rafael Soriano, but I can't quite put my finger on what. I'm afraid thirty-eight-year-old Bob Wickman is too fat but doesn't realize it. Pete Moylan, currently our best middle reliever, was previously a pharmaceutical salesman in Australia.

These issues are representative of the things that haunt me on a day-to-day basis between March and October every year. But I'm a reasonable person, and I'm willing to endure some anxiety. Look, the platoons in left field and at second base are unconventional but they're working, and demoting Chad Paronto from the role of designated ground ball pitcher was smart. I'd been suggesting all of these moves to Bobby Cox for weeks, and now that they're working, I hope he realizes that these were originally my ideas. Right now Bobby and I are getting along great, perhaps the best we've gotten along in many years.

Except for the Chris Woodward situation. For the last two weeks, Woodward, our utility infielder, has been slumping. He has been no help to the Atlanta Braves lately. To my Atlanta Braves. Hey, maybe Woodward will come back around. I hope Woodward can get it going again, and perhaps it's just going to take playing time for that to happen. That seems to be the way Bobby is approaching this. In the meantime, it's killing me. Honestly, I've got heartburn from this.

I understand that sports fans can be partially (if not fully) obsessive. That is part of the deal; a component of the pact that comes along with being a supporter of any team. We feel like we have to be constantly on guard, lest some horrible evil befall our franchise. And, in turn, fall on us. Not to the Braves. Not on my watch.

The thing is, I care vigilantly about every member of the franchise, from the players to the coaches to the front office staff. If the Braves announce the hiring of someone as trivial as a new travel secretary, I will immediately Google him and comb through his work history, looking for gaps in the résumé, as if I'd been charged with hiring him to begin with. Baseball teams often off-load aging players in exchange for younger prospects. Whenever the Braves bring in young guys, I study every bit of information available. They may never set foot on a major league field, but I want and need to know them inside and out. If I don't care, who will? You can't have a championship organization without having first-class people.

So I guess you could say that regarding Chris Woodward, Bobby and I seem to be at an impasse.

But it keeps us going.

Some of us learn from history, some of us from books, some of us from our families, some of us never learn. The thing is, lessons are all around us, just waiting to be absorbed. It's all about where you look to learn. Even if you're not really looking to learn.

During the mid-to-late 1990s, when my friend Matt and I were in our early twenties, we watched *The Jerry Springer Show* every afternoon. Our daily schedule involved watching *Springer* and then playing Madden for a few hours. Then fast food for dinner. Then sports on TV. Then Madden again before bed. I will allow that we probably could have been more productive members of society. I like to think that we were pacing ourselves.

For a while there, everything in our lives revolved around *Springer*. We mostly appreciated the sheer inanity of it all. We'd tune in and then sit sipping from our cans of Mountain Dew, and we'd cheer for these poor, sad people who were perhaps irrationally afraid of zippers, or maybe suspicious they had been impregnated by a goat in their sleep. These guests would confront their issues on national television, speak about them calmly and rationally, begin yelling at another guest, and then, unpredictably but reliably, a brawl would break out.

The Jerry Springer Show was billed as a reflection of a larger slice of society than television had ever shown us before, a fascinating, sometimes disturbing look deep into the fringes of our culture. People relegated to the American moral minority, the sort of folk who were serially engaged in things like promiscuity, deceitfulness, drug abuse, prejudice, and crime—usually simultaneously—were suddenly revealed to the rest of us. And we, the people, embraced them. *Springer* was terribly popular: by 1998, it was averaging around seven million viewers per episode.

Being able to identify myself as a *Springer* viewer was like being in a biker gang or getting a tattoo: it was about as badass as I could get. Living in the Bible Belt, the son of Southern Baptists, I could only rebel stealthily. I didn't drink, mostly hung around the apartment, and lived by the old Southern adage "Don't smoke, don't chew, and don't go with girls who do." But if watching a TV show could guarantee me entrée into a new social class, that much I could handle. Maybe watching *Springer* didn't make me "cool," but it certainly identified me as someone who wasn't afraid to watch imbeciles fight.

I came to *Jerry Springer* something of a moralist who believed that because of my lifestyle, I was clearly a better person than those who did not live the way I did, a group that included pretty much every person involved with *The Jerry Springer Show*. But watching *Springer* made me more forgiving of those living alternative or nontraditional lifestyles. I often felt empathy, if not sympathy, for these people. Before long, I realized I wasn't better than them, and they weren't worse than me; we were just different. We'd been dealt different lives, and we were all just trying to make the best of what was around. Even though I'd been raised to believe that all people were equal, it took *Jerry Springer* to show me what that really means.

I also learned that if anyone ever invites you to Chicago to appear on a TV program because they would like to reveal something to you, you probably should ask if it wouldn't better be handled in private. The free trip might be nice and all, but I've been to Chicago; having your shirt ripped off and your hair pulled out on national television definitely isn't worth getting to stand on the concrete shores of Lake Michigan.

In other words, I learned a lot from *Jerry Springer*. But these days my life is mostly informed by a series of principles I have fortuitously extracted from Atlanta Braves manager Bobby Cox, who couldn't be more opposite from Jerry Springer if he tried to be.

Sports fans seem to know about Bobby Cox in an especially general sense: Braves manager for over two decades, fourth-winningest manager in the history of Major League Baseball, once was involved in an unsavory domestic dispute, gets thrown out of games often. Beyond that, and despite his undeniable success, Bobby Cox remains something of a mystery to many sports fans, even dedicated baseball fans. To begin with, the national media don't pay him much mind, and Cox seems to prefer it that way. He doesn't endorse any products. He refuses to do those in-game interviews during nationally televised games. He's never released an autobiography ghostwritten by a sportswriter buddy. In this era where sports figures always seem to be looking to diversify their brand and make another buck,

Cox is the anomaly: a person preoccupied with simply doing his job as best he can. If this means there's a slight disconnect between Cox and the general public, that seems to be just fine with Bobby.

So you may be wondering how I was able to develop such a close relationship with Bobby Cox. If he is so focused on baseball, how would a guy half his age who lives in Manhattan, almost nine hundred miles from Atlanta, be able to absorb his considerable wisdom?

I've never sat at Bobby's cleats and soaked in a series of homespun maxims while Cox chomped on a cigar, but I do know him. I know him very well, actually—very, very well—and we have an active, totally participatory relationship. I watch nearly every Atlanta Braves game, which means that for a conservative estimate, just over the last decade I've seen Bobby manage well over 1,000 baseball games. And Bobby's always the same. At this point, I know what moves he's going to make before he makes them, which as a Braves fan is a bit disconcerting, because I'm guessing that opposing managers, who have vast networks of scouts and analysts working for them, can predict Bobby's next move as well.

But the Braves kept winning: Cox accumulated 2,504 victories. Since 1991, the Braves under Cox won more games than they lost in every season except one. This gave Cox the highest winning percentage of any active manager in baseball at the end of his career. He's won as many league pennants as Tony LaRussa and one fewer than Joe Torre—the two contemporary managers in Bobby's class—but Cox has only won one World Series ring, compared to LaRussa's two and Torre's four. For as many seasons as the Braves were dominant over the rest of the National League, they were officially the best team in all of baseball only once. As good as Cox was, some Braves fans think that winning just a single World Series in twenty seasons means Bobby wasn't quite good enough.

Though I watch many of the Braves' weeknight games on a self-imposed tape delay, battling sleep and trying my best to concentrate on every pitch, I'll admit that I'm usually online or writing or doing other stuff at the same time. As much as I love the Braves, it's impossible to be as obsessive as I'd like to be and be a fully productive human with a job and a life.

But Sunday is our day, my chance for some alone time with Bobby. My wife knows that Sunday afternoons are reserved for the Braves, and to not even bother asking me to walk the dog or take out the trash. I never ask her to skip a meeting with her shrink, and she doesn't ask me to skip a session with Bobby. On those Sundays, I pull up the curtains and let the sun shine in. I stretch out on the couch, crank up the air conditioning, grab a blanket, and cuddle with Starbury. I can't tell you how much I look forward to those Sunday afternoons. Bobby is my sanity. I take the remote control and a bottle of Coke, and that's really all I need. For the next three hours, I am in a trance, breaking it only to remind Bobby to pinch-hit, maybe suggesting a hit-and-run or a pitchout now and then, but mostly it's Bobby and me, sitting shoulder to shoulder in my imaginary Braves dugout, watching the games go by.

This is now the story of my baseball life. I moved from Atlanta to New York City in the summer of 2000, and I quickly found that following the Braves while living in Manhattan is nearly as easy as following them from Atlanta. Every game is on TV, and the internet provides all the news and rumors I could ever need. Upon arriving in New York, I thought about casually pulling for the Yankees, just so I could become part of a local fan base and have, you know, human interactions with a cabal of like-minded followers. But the Braves, if anything, have only tightened their grip on me since I left town.

I suppose it's partially because of the isolation. I'm in the heart of New York Mets country, the Braves' archrival, so I'm subjected to taunts and insults as I walk the streets wearing my Braves hats and jerseys. As I often point out to my coworkers and friends who are Mets fans, Bobby's tenure hasn't been kind to them. There's not much room for Mets fans to talk, but that doesn't seem to stop any of them. And then there are the Yankees fans, who seem, at best, to pity the team their team beat in the 1996 and 1999 World Series, usurping a would-be dynasty.

Stranded here on this island with my Braves, I've adopted something of a foxhole mentality. We are in this together: Bobby, the players, and me. Whether they know it or not, they need me as much as I need them. Because if I don't watch every game, if I don't stand and cheer in my living room, if I don't work the home plate umpire, if I don't call out suggestions at the televised image of Bobby Cox, the Braves just might fall completely apart.

Baseball teams in the modern era have plenty of turnover. Whereas players in the fifties, sixties, and early seventies often spent most of their careers on the same team, these days free agency and the constant search for another sizable payday ensure that most guys are never going to find a home. Back in 1998 and 1999, the Braves got several months of good work from a relief pitcher named Russ Springer. Braves fans were just starting to warm to him when the season ended. Springer left the Braves soon after and was still in the majors in 2010, at forty-one years old, with the Cincinnati Reds, his tenth major league team in eighteen seasons. He was also with Houston, St. Louis, and Arizona twice, among others. Did he ever develop an enduring following in any of those cities along the way? No, though not because he lacked talent or personality; it was because he never stayed with one franchise long enough for the fans to embrace him. It's hard to give people hugs when they won't stand still.

Defying all of that, Bobby Cox spent twenty consecutive seasons as the manager of the Atlanta Braves. He outlasted every player, coach, front office exec, television commentator, television station, and even a fifty-thousand-seat stadium. Bobby is our rock, our fortress, our shield, our comfort, our salvation. He may be rickety and a bit of a curmudgeon at sixty-nine, but Bobby's presence alone lends stability. Not only to the team but also to me. We can't rely on much in life, but I know Bobby will be there for me day after day, week after week, month after month, year after year. Over those twenty seasons, I've hated Bobby, loved him, praised him, even publicly denounced him. Now I can't imagine my life without him. Bobby Cox has been the single most important person in my sporting life.

And in getting to know him and the players he has molded, following the Braves through their run winning an unprecedented fourteen consecutive division titles from 1991 through 2005 and a World Championship, I've learned a few things along the way.

CHAPTER 1

EMOTION: How Greg Maddux Is Like Traveling Cross-Country with Your Grandparents

During the 1990 baseball season, Atlanta Braves rookie David Justice stepped into the batter's box in a game against the Chicago Cubs. An unassuming twenty-four-year-old named Greg Maddux was pitching. Maddux was in his fifth season with Chicago, where he'd already established himself as one of baseball's best young pitchers, as well as a rather gentlemanly sort.

According to a story reported by *Sports Illustrated* a few years later, when Justice stepped up to the plate, Maddux made eye contact and mouthed the words, "— you." Justice gestured at Maddux as if to say, "Um, are you talking to me?" Maddux mimicked the gesture back at Justice.

Justice, who did not know Maddux personally and had never had any previous interactions with him, was genuinely surprised by this. Justice was a hot-shot rookie, and while Maddux had pitched in one All-Star Game and finished third in the previous year's National League Cy Young Award voting, this was

Greg Maddux, a man who looked better suited to advise high school students on the college application process than to stand on a mound mouthing profane taunts at the sleek power hitter who a few months later would be named Rookie of the Year and who two years later would marry actress Halle Berry.

After perplexing and infuriating Justice, Maddux got him out. The following day, Justice arrived at the stadium early, rounded up a posse of Braves players, and went looking for Maddux to exact some sort of revenge. To his credit, Maddux displayed the same ability to outthink hitters that he would utilize throughout his twenty-three-year career: he was nowhere to be found.

Two years later, the Braves signed Maddux as a free agent. Justice had been so angry since the 1990 incident that he'd steered clear of Maddux since, and his plan was to continue to do so once Maddux arrived at Atlanta's spring training camp in West Palm Beach. Instead Maddux showed up, walked directly to Justice, and introduced himself by saying, "Hey, Dave, how bad did you want to kick my ass?"

"And all the frustration and anger seemed to disappear," Justice told *SI.* "We laughed, and now I'd walk through a wall for Greg Maddux. I like the way he plays the game."

Pretty much everyone did. John Smoltz once said that Maddux made his opponents look like they were swinging foam bats, while former Cy Young Award winner Dwight Gooden said of him, "You wish there was another league he could get called up to." With 355 wins, a .610 winning percentage, and four consecutive NL Cy Young Awards, Greg Maddux was quite possibly the greatest pitcher of all time. And for the majority of that time, Maddux was an Atlanta Brave under Bobby Cox.

In that way, simply because of his longevity and not because of any philosophical managerial ethos, Bobby is the connective tissue for the Braves' players. So many of them have rotated through Atlanta, some for a few months, some for a few years. They all wore the hat with the stylized *A*, and they all played for Bobby Cox. Bobby's overarching presence is like the rug in *The Big Lebowski*: he really ties the room together.

The Braves signed Greg Maddux as a free agent after the 1992 season, in which they had gone 98–64 and lost the World Series to the Toronto Blue Jays, for their second consecutive World Series loss. Atlanta's pitching rotation had two budding stars in John Smoltz, who was twenty-five at the time, and twenty-game winner Tom Glavine, who was twenty-six. Steve Avery, only twenty-two years old, also looked promising, having gone 11–11 and logged a substantial 233 innings. The right-handed Maddux, twenty-six, had won his first Cy Young Award, but the Braves outbid the Cubs and everyone else and signed him to a contract that was then considered outrageously lavish: five years, $28 million. The Yankees, who'd endured four consecutive losing seasons and were trying to rebuild, actually offered him more money; Maddux turned it down to join Atlanta's budding dynasty.

Maddux combined with Smoltz and Glavine to form the core of the Braves' pitching staff for the next decade. As Steve Avery's career acceded to injury, others were sprinkled in as fourth and fifth starters: Kent Mercker, Jason Schmidt, Kevin Millwood, Dennis Martinez, Bruce Chen, John Burkett, Damian Moss, Jason Marquis, and Denny Neagle.

In conversation, it was usually Maddux, Glavine, and Smoltz. The positioning of the names Smoltz and Glavine was almost interchangeable in that phrase, but Maddux always came first. This is because he was the best pitcher the Braves have ever had. As Bobby Cox said when Maddux retired in 2009: "I get asked by managers and press people all the time, how good was he? Was he the best pitcher I ever saw? Was he the smartest pitcher I ever saw? Was he the best competitor I ever saw? Was he the best teammate I ever saw? The answer is yes to all the above."

During his first three seasons in Atlanta, Maddux won the Cy Young Award each season. In his transcendent 1997 campaign, Maddux pitched 232 innings and faced 893 batters, and he unintentionally walked just 14 of them. He did not throw a wild pitch the entire season, and he finished the year with 19 wins and 4 losses. In one complete game win at Wrigley Field that season, Maddux needed to throw only 76 pitches over 9 innings, and 63 of those pitches were strikes. Between 1997 and 2000, perhaps his best run despite not winning any Cy Young Awards, Maddux totaled 75 wins against 31 losses, with a 2.73 ERA and 24 complete games. Maddux won more games during the 1990s than any other pitcher in baseball. He won at least 15 games for 17 consecutive seasons. He won the Gold Glove Award 18 times.

We got to watch this man pitch every fifth day, and watching Maddux informed me as a fan. It was through studying him that I grasped pitching as art form, the importance of matching craft and guile with equal parts determination and intensity. These qualities were so important to Maddux, it was almost as though he subsisted on them entirely. His pitch speeds were average at best, and he wasn't able to supplement his speed with an arsenal of trick pitches or wacky deliveries. What Maddux did have, though, was precise control of and tremendous movement on pretty much every pitch he threw. He couldn't whip the ball past you, but he could *budge* it by you by placing it exactly where you were least expecting it. And sometimes even where you were expecting it.

As soon as a left-handed hitter had two strikes on him, Maddux would zing a two-seam fastball across the inside corner of the plate. He did this with 1,000 percent regularity. If Maddux got to a two-strike count on twenty-five left-handed batters during a game, his next pitch to all twenty-five guys would be a two-seam fastball on the inside corner.

The two-seam fastball is different from the pitch commonly known as the fastball. The fastball is technically a *four-seam* fastball, so named because of the way the pitcher, when releasing the pitch, aligns his index and middle fingers so that they are perpendicular across all four of the baseball's seams. Upon release of the ball, this produces a spin that gives the baseball a nearly straight path to the plate. In contrast, the two-seam fastball is thrown with the pitcher's middle and index fingers running parallel to two of the seams, which, for reasons known only to physicists and pitching coaches, makes the ball jump abruptly in the final five to ten feet before it reaches the plate.

Maddux perfected a two-seam fastball that he threw somewhere between eighty-six and eighty-eight miles per hour. The ball looked, at least as it was being released from Maddux's hand, as though it were coming straight in on the hands of left-handed batters. The hitters would reflexively raise their arms, jolting the bat high over their head and removing their arms and hands from the path of the ball. The ball was definitely going to hit them; if they moved, they not only wouldn't get hit but there was also no way it could possibly be a strike. Then, just as the batters were committed to not being able to swing at the pitch, Maddux's two-seamer would zip three to four inches back to his right, away from the batter, just catching the corner of the plate for a called strike three.

Maddux pitching + left-handed hitter + two strikes + two-seam fastball = called third strike on the inside corner of the plate. I can't tell you how many times I saw the various integers in that equation add up to the same result. Five hundred times? One thousand times? And unless the entire group of Major League Baseball players and coaches are by some miracle dumber than I am, surely they all knew this pitch was coming.

So why did it work so effectively and so consistently? Obviously, it was partially effective because Maddux was taking advantage of the hitter's instincts and training. Hitters have worked their entire lives to condition their bodies to read and react. They see a pitch coming down the middle, they swing. They see a pitch coming at their hands, they get their hands out of the way. Maddux slung the ball, they recognized a ball coming in on their hands, they moved their hands out of the way. And then the pitch did what it wasn't supposed to be able to do: it made a 90-degree turn away from them and over the back corner of the plate.

Watching Maddux pitch, you'd see hitter after hitter leave the field shaking his head, consumed with disgust and incredulity. On the mound with a baseball in his hand, Greg Maddux was a genius, or as close to genius as I believe I'll ever see. Stories abound of Maddux thinking not one pitch ahead but sometimes two or three pitches ahead. According to a 1995 *Sports Illustrated* cover story, on one of his off days, he was sitting next to Smoltz in the Braves dugout and studying the game in progress. Four different times, Maddux predicted the batter was imminently going to foul off a pitch that would come streaking into the dugout. Three of the four times, Maddux was correct.

Maddux's beautiful mind was cloaked in a completely pedestrian build. While much of baseball in the nineties was discovering performance-enhancing drugs and inflating themselves into unrecognizable he-men, Maddux looked as though he was a cubicle worker who'd won a contest and was being allowed to start a Major League Baseball game thanks to promotional support from Dr Pepper.

My favorite Maddux story occurred during the 1999 season. Throughout his time with the Braves, Maddux continuously wore glasses whenever he wasn't pitching. He went through several models, evolving a few years behind whatever the current fashion was, and some might have concluded that the glasses made him look like a dork. Maddux had trouble with contacts—it was often reported that he was allergic to contacts, though Maddux once said he merely had "bumpy eyes"—but he didn't feel comfortable pitching while wearing glasses. So he'd wear the lenses for the hour or two he was pitching, once every five days, and then he wore glasses the rest of the time.

Maddux started the '99 season slowly, compiling a tolerable 6–5 record over his first 15 starts, and for the first time in five years he wasn't invited to pitch in the midseason All-Star Game. Maddux took advantage of the free weekend to get LASIK surgery on his eyes, and then—less than forty-eight hours after allowing lasers to slice tiny cuts on his eyeballs, potentially ruining not only his vision but the Braves' season with a completely elective and, at that time, still new surgical procedure—Maddux started an interleague game against the Boston Red Sox and allowed one run over eight innings. He finished the year 19–9.

When the Associated Press asked him why he had the surgery, Maddux explained, "I was tired of being a dork."

I wasn't exactly a dork growing up, but I wasn't cool, either. My life was about as normal as could be; completely unremarkable by most standards. By contrast, Carl Alfred Edfeldt was born to Swedish immigrants above a general store in tiny Robertsdale, Alabama, in 1915. After marrying Carolyn Baker in 1939, Edfeldt put himself through business college and then served six years in the navy during World War II, moving to Chicago and San Francisco to work out of bases in each city. When the war ended, he moved back to Alabama, bought some farmland in the country south of Birmingham, and settled there with his burgeoning family, which by then included three daughters, one of whom would eventually become my mother. Carl—or as I called him, Paw Paw—worked almost forty years for the United States Postal Service until he retired in 1976. Nothing in his life was given to him; he created it all from scratch. I've always thought that was about as admirable as it gets.

My cousin Jill and I are the oldest grandkids in our family, and when we reached an age my grandparents deemed appropriate, Paw Paw and my grandmother, Nana Carolyn, decided they would show us the United States. Every summer, they promised that the four of us—Nana, Paw Paw, Jill, and I— would embark on a fantastical road trip.

In 1982 my grandparents decided to begin our travels by taking me and Jill to visit the World's Fair. I later learned that the first World's Fair was proposed by Prince Albert, husband of Queen Victoria, as an exhibition of products manufactured around the world. In 1982, pre-internet, World's Fairs still served an important purpose, showing ordinary citizens technological advances happening around the globe that might otherwise go unchecked. At the '82 World's Fair, for instance, I tasted milk that could be stored in a box, unrefrigerated. As soon as it hit my lips, I knew it would never work—it tasted like metal, not milk. They could've saved a lot of money just by checking with me on my way out.

There must be a reason that Knoxville, Tennessee, was awarded the 1982 World's Fair, but I can't figure out what it was. The previous World's Fairs had taken place in grand cities like Paris and New York and Brussels. To its credit, Knoxville accepted the challenge, attempting to present itself to a worldwide audience as something more than a college town. As if to prove its worth, the city of Knoxville constructed a 266-foot tower with a dimpled golden globe at the top and named it the Sunsphere. A few weeks after the World's Fair opened, early one morning before everything opened for the day, someone fired a single gunshot into the Sunsphere. That person was never caught.

Whoever did it probably could have pled temporary insanity due to the World's Fair theme song. Down in Atlanta, we'd been subject for months to a steady stream of 1982 World's Fair commercials. These ads, now gloriously memorialized on YouTube, were like early works by director Michael Bay, with gratuitous smiling shots of international faces and ridiculous special effects. The ad ended with the Space Shuttle *Columbia* being cleared to land not at an air force base but in Knoxville— I guess when the Space Shuttle descends from the lower thermosphere at eighteen thousand miles per hour, landing on a commuter airport runway is a totally viable option—and the astronauts telling mission control, "We've got to be there!" A chorus of studio singers then practically shouted, "You've got to *beeeeeeeeeeeeee* . . . there!" Jill says she remembers me singing this in the car the entire way to Knoxville. I can't deny that I might have done this.

The next summer, we drove to St. Louis, and the next year to Washington, DC. The year after that, we took a train to New York City; dealing with a station wagon in Manhattan didn't seem to be a prudent idea, even to my station wagon–obsessed grandfather. (Years later, he would grudgingly convert to the minivan.) On the train to New York, we had side-by-side roomettes. Each had two seats facing each other. At night these folded together to simulate a single bed—well, a single bed with a gap in the middle of it—and there was also a pull-down bunk bed above the seats. There wasn't space for a shower, but there was a small steel sink in the corner and a toilet that folded out from the wall and into the room, as though we were in a mobile prison cell.

On our ride up to New York, Jill and I opted to share a roomette. We played cards, read, whatever, then eventually bunked down for the night. I was sleeping well, lulled into a peaceful slumber by the gentle locomotion of the train, when Jill woke me up to inform me she needed to pee and that I should not open my eyes. Obviously, I wouldn't have opened my eyes while I was sleeping, but now that I was awake, I agreed not to look, and I rolled over to gaze out the window at the Eastern Seaboard whizzing past in the moonlight.

I listened as the toilet was folded down, and then flushed soon after. I heard the sink turn on and then off, then felt Jill scrambling back into her upper bunk bed. A few minutes later, just as I was drifting back to sleep, I reached down to pull up my blanket and found it was splattered with a warm liquid. I recoiled my hand with alacrity, as if I were reaching for my pistol in a duel. The folding toilet obviously wasn't a very stable contraption; it was easy to imagine Jill struggling with it, her accuracy compromised. I relegated myself to spending the night shivering, the blanket bunched around my ankles, untouched. The next morning, after thawing out, without explaining why I was curious, I asked Jill if using the toilet the previous evening had been tough. Not particularly, she reported. Although, she mentioned, the water from the sink had given her some difficulty, splattering all over the place.

In New York City, I don't remember where we stayed or what we did, other than visiting the Statue of Liberty, where the wind on Ellis Island repeatedly dislodged Paw Paw's highly hair-sprayed comb-over, flipping it straight up into the air, like a lid opening atop his head. He eventually bought an adjustable Yankees cap to remedy the situation. Paw Paw was more a college football fan than a baseball fan, but when the street vendor offered him the choice between the Mets or the Yankees, he chose the Yankees. At least he had class.

When Greg Maddux arrived in Atlanta, watching him pitch on TBS for the first few months was like having a front row seat at a 2 Live Crew concert. Maddux was clearly a master of two things: controlling his pitches and cursing. After pretty much every pitch that was either called a ball or hit harder or farther than Maddux expected, the TBS on-field microphones would catch him screaming a profanity. It was usually one word, sometimes two, but always a wicked selection that I'm sure had people all over the Bible Belt scrambling for the mute button. This went on for at least his first season with the Braves, until someone, perhaps from the Federal Communications Commission or the TBS Standards and Practices Division, apparently gave him a talking-to. Maddux eventually managed to mostly curb the cursing, though his head would still snap with a silent vulgarity after he made a mistake.

More than anything, the right-hander wanted to win. His nickname became "Doggie," short for "Mad Dog," which not only shared alliteration with "Maddux" and was ironic when contrasted to his subdued look but mostly represented his tenacity about winning. He may not have always looked like a guy completely invested in winning games, but he definitely sounded like one.

With Maddux, I always appreciated that sentiment, if not the expression. It showed us that he cared, he really, really cared. Maddux wanted to be perfect, and when he wasn't, even just once, it angered him, deeply and audibly. And I loved that. Thinking back, I have no memories of Maddux celebrating. Goodness knows he rang up enough strikeouts and other big plays to have had the opportunity. He just never did. No fist pumps, no pointing at batters. Maddux was more focused on the pursuit of perfection. He would not settle for being great, he wanted to be the greatest. If the only way he could do this was with a sailor's vocabulary, I could live with it. We could turn down the volume. Hitters couldn't get away from the two-seamer.

Before the 2004 season, after eleven seasons with the Braves, Maddux became a free agent and signed with the Chicago Cubs, the team that first brought him to the majors. He pitched five more seasons in the majors, staying in the National League and bouncing between Chicago, Los Angeles, and San Diego, clearing over $40 million total. He was on a decline during this time, losing a few miles per hour off each pitch, losing a few inches off his location, and he went a combined 66–64 with a 4.16 ERA. He was still effective, just not $9-million-a-year effective.

Maddux didn't retire as a member of the Braves, which bothered me, but that seems to be the Atlanta way. When players get older and their price tags begin to reflect their history more than their future, the Braves are content to let them go elsewhere. The franchise doesn't want to pay for nostalgia, because although it might sell a few tickets, it doesn't win games. This may be a sound business model, but it makes for some awkward sights, such as a latter-day Greg Maddux laboring hard in a deeply unflattering khaki Padres uniform.

When Maddux was inducted into the Braves Hall of Fame in the summer of 2009, Chipper Jones recalled his own first opening day in the majors, against the San Francisco Giants in 1995. Maddux got the start for the Braves, and with two outs in the top of the first inning, Barry Bonds came to the plate. Maddux got Bonds to pop the ball up on the infield, and Chipper, fired up on opening day, decided to take charge, so he went galloping across the pitcher's mound to make the catch. While he was focused on the ball, however, he sprinted directly into Greg Maddux, and the two went down in a heap.

According to Chipper, after hitting the grass, the next thing he remembered hearing was Maddux's analysis of the play: "Bleepdammit motherbleeper! Settle the bleep down, you bleeping rookie! Bleep bleep, bleep bleep!" (Those were Chipper's bleeps, not mine.)

At the end of the Braves Hall of Fame ceremony honoring him, Maddux took the microphone and delivered a calm, unemotional speech. He ended it in a serene monotone by saying, "Thank you for having me and . . . let's crush the Mets tonight, huh? Let's get 'em."

A few hours later, the Braves beat the Mets 11–0.

Not long after our New York train excursion, we learned that the trip had actually been a test run. The next summer, my grandparents were going all-out. This time they also invited my younger sister, Claire, and Jill's younger brother, Baker, along, and we set off to see America's West via train. The six of us began in Alabama, driving across Mississippi and down to New Orleans. My grandfather left the station wagon in an ultra-secure long-term parking lot in downtown New Orleans, and we piled aboard an Amtrak train pointed west.

My grandparents had booked one large room for each leg of the journey, a sole compartment that was alleged to sleep four. It had a large sleeper sofa along one wall, as well as a bunk bed that folded down from the ceiling. Baker and Claire had to be about nine years old, and they were small enough to share the top bunk. The couch extended into a double bed, which my grandmother would alternate sharing each evening with either me or Jill. We also had four reserved seats in the adjoining passenger car, where my grandfather and either me or Jill would have two seats apiece on which to sleep fitfully every night.

It took a few days, but we chugged across lower Texas, New Mexico, and Arizona. It was fun being on the train, at least when we were all still excited by the novelty of being on a train and hadn't yet grown to resent feeling trapped. From what I observed, people who chose to travel on trains back in the mid-1980s seemed to be doing it by necessity rather than choice; they either looked as though they couldn't afford plane tickets, or maybe they were afraid to fly. Any romance of the rails was erased every time I walked into one of the passenger cars, because they all smelled like feet.

Our room on the train had a toilet/shower. The slash there is key, as it serves to indicate that things done in the toilet and things done in the shower were supposed to both be accomplished within the same space. It was a small square built out into the room, with a door that latched open and closed from the inside. The interior of the bathroom was coated in a single smooth layer of plastic, and there were really only four interactive things in the bathroom:

1. The toilet
2. The toilet lid
3. A button to flush the toilet
4. A button that triggered the shower

Amtrak's definition of a shower differed radically from mine. Its shower was a spigot embedded in the ceiling of the bathroom. Once the "on" button was hit, the shower ran for exactly three minutes, and it was set at a predetermined nine thousand degrees—an unscientific guesstimate, but I'm still physically and mentally scarred, so it must be close. One try was enough for me; after that, I waited until we were in cities between train segments to bathe.

One afternoon, Baker stepped into the bathroom for a

quick pee. When he finished, he turned and hit the flush button, except he actually pressed the shower button. Those of us sitting just outside in the room heard the shower click on and exchanged looks of horror. Baker apparently tried to make an initial escape, as the door briefly opened a few inches before it stopped moving; boiling water immediately started splashing out into the room. We couldn't see Baker, so we assumed he'd either melted or instantly had managed to press himself up against the back wall, mostly out of the way of the water, but effectively trapping himself until the shower's timer ran out. From somewhere back behind the water, over the *rat-a-tat* of the hellfire shower, Baker's poor, small voice cried out, "It's hot!"

We arrived in Los Angeles and immediately transferred onto a train headed up the California coast toward the Bay Area. We stayed for three days in San Francisco, taking a day trip out to Yosemite National Park. From San Francisco we Amtraked up to Seattle, then on to Vancouver for a day, then back to Seattle, where we caught another train heading back east to Chicago.

We were supposed to have maybe a half-day layover in Chicago, and I was hoping we'd have time to get to a Cubs game. I'd just recently started watching baseball, and the Cubs were always on WGN. When my parents first got cable TV, it was as if they'd bought a rocket ship to Mars. Instead of having six channels, we now had a mind-boggling thirty! The cable box had ten buttons and a switcher that moved you from the 1 to 10 tier, to channels 11 to 20 and to the 21 to 30 bands. The Braves were on TV most nights, and I'd either sit and watch the games with my parents, or I'd run next door and watch with my next-door neighbor, an elderly woman named Mrs. Osbourne who loved the Braves. (Although we could watch the game only after we'd watched *Wheel of Fortune* and *Family Feud*.) When we got cable, I soon realized that the Cubs were on almost every afternoon, so I became a nominal fan of those early eighties Cubs teams with Ryne Sandberg, Leon Durham, Lee Smith, Ron Cey, and Bump Wills. This was exactly when I was first falling in love with the Braves, and I found it impossible to divide my loyalties. But the Cubs introduced me to the ineffable romance of baseball, with Wrigley Field's ivy-covered wall, the row houses just beyond the outfield, and a blustery announcer name Harry Carey, whose son, Skip, I eventually deduced, was calling Braves games in a style all his own.

Unfortunately, as our train set out toward Chicago, we were delayed for a few hours late one night just after leaving Denver and didn't make it to Chicago in time for the game.

After just over two weeks on the road, we returned to New Orleans and found the station wagon in perfect condition for the ride back to Alabama. Before that trip, I had envisioned myself peering out of the window as we traversed the mesas and plateaus of the American Southwest, seeing the morning fog roll in off San Francisco Bay, taking in the greenery of the Pacific Northwest, reflecting upon the Rocky Mountains as the sun rose in the distance. It's not that I didn't see amazing things—all of those sights were things I actually observed—but they weren't the revelatory experiences I was expecting them to be, or perhaps that I was hoping they would be.

During the station wagon journeys, if we stumbled upon any sort of historic site or tourist attractions along the way—battlefields, Elvis's birthplace, interesting rock formations—Nana would gently try to convince Paw Paw that we should stop. Paw Paw would always not-so-gently disagree with these suggestions, insisting that we were already hopelessly behind schedule and under no circumstances could we endure any more delays. Shoot, he'd snort, we'll be lucky if we can find time to stop for gas, much less see the tallest waterfall in southeastern Indiana.

"Carl . . ," Nana would reply, the ellipsis a passive-aggressive dig designed to worm its way into his subconscious.

A few minutes later, we'd be looking at the tallest waterfall in southeastern Indiana while my grandmother, a retired high school teacher, delivered an impromptu lecture about how waterfalls were formed. Paw Paw would usually wait by the car, tapping his foot, checking his watch.

When Bobby Cox gets truly angry—and I mean profoundly furious, not just perturbed—his tell is his hat. Bobby gets upset when an umpire blows a call, but he reserves his most authentic anger for players who don't follow orders. During a game in the 2009 season, with Yunel Escobar at the plate and a runner on base, Cox called for a hit-and-run. The pitch was a little inside, and instead of swinging to protect the runner, Escobar ducked back, as though the pitch was about to hit him. Instead it swerved across the plate for a called strike, and the runner was thrown out at second. The broadcast cameras immediately cut to Cox, who had already removed his hat and was cursing loudly. I don't know where the phrase "flip his lid" comes from, but it certainly applies in a literal way to Bobby.

My grandfather was a person to whom time was very important; first and foremost, in everything he did, he was always punctual. I'm not sure if that's because he was a postman, or if he was a postman because he was punctual, but either way it must have been a great fit. Paw Paw equated punctuality with respect, something I learned from him. If you are meeting me at nine in the morning, I will be there at nine in the morning. If my wife says she'll be ready to leave for dinner in ten minutes, I will be waiting at the door, checking my watch and tapping my foot, in exactly ten minutes. If you can't be ready at the agreed-upon time we both said we would be ready, please let me know in advance. Either way, there are few things I appreciate more than you not wasting my time.

Paw Paw lived his entire life on time. Time wasn't money, it was something more important. One Saturday a few years ago, I drove from Atlanta to Alabama to spend a day with him. The trip normally took about two and a half hours each way, but I stopped halfway to do something important, like buy fireworks, and I arrived at his farm maybe a half hour later than he was expecting me. When I pulled up in the driveway, he was sitting out front on the porch, wearing his houndstooth University of Alabama hat. The first thing he said to me: "Hey!" The second thing he said to me: "Did you get lost?"

The moment we fell behind on one of our trips, Paw Paw would almost visibly tense up. He wouldn't speed along the highway, but he would get a little more aggressive in tone, maybe a bit more proactive. He was a Christian man, so he didn't curse, but he could occasionally adopt a character that was a little jarring. I didn't like that Paw Paw, so I did everything in my power not to make him angry. My grandmother, however, was never scared, and she did not hesitate to poke the angry lion. They would bicker and argue, always politely, but both resolute in getting their way.

I recall once asking my grandmother if she and my grandfather would ever get a divorce. Never, she assured me. Then why, I asked, did they fight so often? They weren't fighting, she calmly explained, they were just discussing things. She said that once you get to know someone really well, when you truly loved someone, you can be honest with each other. They weren't concerned about hurting feelings, they just wanted to get their points across.

And win the argument, of course.

It wasn't until many years later that I understood the actual value of expressing myself. And it was watching Bobby Cox manage the Braves that rammed this home.

Cox is the loudest baseball manager I've ever heard. He spends a great deal of time exhorting his players from the dugout when they're at bat, yelping things like "C'mon, Chip!" before almost every swing when Chipper Jones is at the plate. He calls every player by an unofficial nickname that's a shortened version of one of the player's actual names: Adam LaRoche was "Roachey," Andruw Jones was "Andy." And so on. Some players with unusual names are assigned the more generic "C'mon, kid!" I think Bobby uses this because it's easier to say "kid" than it is finding an appropriate contraction for a name like Kenshin Kawakami.

Bobby is, famously, the all-time leader in managerial ejections, yet I don't see his tirades as true showings of emotion but more as premeditated theater—over-the-top exhibitionism designed to elicit a response from the umpires. Is Bobby expressing a genuine feeling in those moments? Sure, but he's expressing it in a hyperbolic way.

But the rest of the time, all those yells and bleats from the dugout between plays and bad calls, that's the real Bobby, or at least who I choose to see as the real Bobby. As rote as his cheerleading is, it is at some level a genuine expression of sentiment, an authentic desire to see his players do their best. I watch a lot of baseball, and I don't ever recall hearing any other manager as consistently vocal and as honestly expressive as Bobby is. He truly, deeply cares about how every player on his team performs. What separates Bobby from the rest of the major league managers is that he's not afraid to be overheard letting his players— and anyone watching a Braves game, actually—know it.

Showing emotion doesn't come naturally to me, whether it's offering simple words of encouragement to someone or trying to get a point across to my wife. When confronted with any situation, my natural tendency is to sit back, ruminate, to let peace and perspective prevail over possible conflict and immediacy. Psychologists would probably call this avoidance. But I've tried to work on it, day by day. My grandparents showed me how way back when, and the shrink I've been seeing since 1990, Bobby Cox, reinforces the lesson.

I know because he tells me all the time. And that matters. "C'mon, kid!"

CHAPTER 2

FAITH: How Greg Norton Is Like
Playing on a Terrible Basketball Team

For as long as Bobby Cox has managed the Braves, one tradition has tragically endured: keeping at least one player on the roster who is having a below-average season. And not only keeping this player on the roster but giving him regular, meaningful, occasionally inexplicable playing time. I touched on Chris Woodward earlier, but there have been plenty more Braves whose presence on my television screen gave me acid reflux. These guys are always position players, veterans, and journeymen, who, for at least one season, found themselves a home under the watchful eye of a manager who finally appreciated them.

Behold one man's list:

> 1991: Tommy Gregg—At twenty-seven years old, Gregg played in 72 games, had 120 at bats, and batted .187.
> 1992: Damon Berryhill—The twenty-eight-year-old catcher played in 101 games but batted .228, with 328 plate appearances and only 17 walks.

1993: Rafael Belliard—At thirty-one years old, the diminutive Raffy was used as a defensive replacement. He played in 91 games but had only 89 plate appearances, in which he had 13 singles, 5 doubles, and nothing else.

1994: Dave Gallagher—He didn't smash melons, but he might as well have. He played in 89 games and had 177 plate appearances, batting just .224 with 5 doubles and 2 home runs.

1995: Rafael Belliard—Playing a bit more regularly, Belliard had 192 plate appearances over 75 games as a backup middle infielder. He managed just 40 hits (2 doubles, 1 triple) and 28 strikeouts, finishing the season batting .222.

1996: Terry Pendleton—Five years removed from his MVP season, TP was thirty-five years old by 1996. Acquired by the Braves for the stretch run, he played in 42 games and had 177 plate appearances. He batted .204 and had an on-base percentage (OBP) of just .271.

1997: Eddie Perez—The twenty-nine-year-old backup catcher with a conquistador's mustache played in 73 games, had 206 plate appearances, and drew only 10 walks while batting .215.

1998: Tony Graffanino—The twenty-six-year-old led all Braves bench players with 317 plate appearances, but he batted just .211 and struck out about once every 5 at-bats.

1999: Otis Nixon—At age forty, the speedy outfielder played in 84 games and logged 176 plate appearances, hitting a skinny .205 in those games. He was mostly a pinch runner, however, and he did excel in that role, stealing 26 bases in 33 attempts.

2000: Trent Hubbard—I have minimal memory of Trent Hubbard, but at thirty-six years old, he played in 61 games and had 96 plate appearances for a .185 batting average.

2001: Ken Caminiti—With the Braves in need of a first baseman, they picked up this former MVP third baseman who'd been released by the Texas Rangers midway through the season. Atlanta moved Caminiti to first and got him 193 plate appearances. He batted .222 and had but 38 hits versus 44 strikeouts.

2002: Henry Blanco—As Javy Lopez's backup at catcher, Blanco played in 81 games but batted just .204. (Then again, Lopez hit just .233.)

2003: Henry Blanco—He played in fewer games this season and accumulated just 166 plate appearances, but for 2003 Blanco managed to hit only .199.

2004: Mark DeRosa—As a utility man deployed all over the field, DeRosa logged 345 plate appearances and batted .239.

2005: Brian Jordan—Jordan was thirty-eight years old and in his thirteenth major league season, and he hit a respectable .247 for the year. Cox started Jordan in game one of the National League Division Series against Houston. The manager said he wanted a veteran in there. Jordan went 0–3. The Braves lost.

2006: Todd Pratt—At thirty-nine years old, Pratt was brought in to back up and tutor Brian McCann. In 62 games, Pratt batted .207.

2007: Chris Woodward—92 games, 136 at bats, .199 batting average.

2008: Corky Miller—The reserve catcher managed to play in 31 games and accrue 67 plate appearances while hitting—are you ready for this?—.083.

2009: Greg Norton—More on first baseman Norton shortly. But the stats for 2009: in 97 plate appearances, 11 hits, 2 doubles, no home runs, 7 runs batted in, 20 base on balls, 20 strikeouts, .145 average.

2010: Nate McLouth—The center fielder started slow, batting just .175 in the month of April. In June, while chasing a fly ball, McLouth had a violent collision with Jason Heyward, and McLouth suffered a concussion, which sent him to the disabled list for a while. After a stint in the minors, McLouth eventually made it back to the majors, but finished the season batting .190 in 242 at bats.

Not all of these guys had forgettable Major League Baseball careers; Terry Pendleton won the 1991 National League MVP Award, Brian Jordan played over a decade as an important everyday player. But just as we enjoyed the rise of so many players, at some point they began an inexorable slide that wasn't as much fun to watch. In fact, it was often painful.

Perhaps every chain needs a weak link or two. As a sports fan, and as someone who has worked within financial limitations every day of my life, I understand it's impossible to always afford to have the best of everything, just as it's impossible for a baseball team to always have a roster composed of only all-stars and bona fide major league regulars—unless, of course, you are the Yankees or Red Sox or Dodgers or Angels or Mets, for whom the economics of anything don't seem to apply. But even they still always seem to end up with a couple of below-average guys.

Accepting this reality, what I always hope for is that the participation of the below-average guys will remain as limited as possible. Seems reasonable, right? For most of the season, there are twenty-five men on an MLB roster. The majority of the time, the better players get the bulk of the opportunities to produce. But as each game progresses, pitchers get taken out, pinch hitters get used, and, often at the end of games, with the bench depleted, the guy who steps to the plate with a chance to win the game is pretty much the last guy you'd like to see up there. To avoid having their worst hitter at the plate in these situations, many managers will designate a guy as their chosen pinch hitter and save him for key situations throughout the season. Bobby Cox has embraced this strategy over the years, although he often seems to select the wrong guy.

Early in the 2008 season, the Braves basically bought the thirty-five-year-old Greg Norton from the Seattle Mariners. Norton had been around the majors for a decade with five different teams, but he had never been an everyday player. Though he had shown a propensity for drawing walks, he'd never batted above .300. Once he arrived in Atlanta, Norton was immediately plugged in as the Braves' go-to pinch hitter. He wasn't great, but he wasn't awful: batted .246 with a .361 OBP and led the majors with three pinch-hit home runs. The

Braves re-signed him to a one-year deal, and Norton returned in 2009.

Norton's stat line from the 2009 season is reproduced at the beginning of this chapter, and to be honest, I'd prefer to spend as little time as possible dwelling on the details. As a fan, it was one of the more excruciating and inexplicable things I've endured, particularly the regularity of it. As each game ticked along, we knew that Norton was sitting there on the bench waiting to be deployed. While the Braves made a run for the NL East division title late in the 2009 season, Norton had three hits in August and September combined.

It has been said that pinch-hitting is something of an art form. It requires supreme patience and a certain mental clarity. To be successful, a pinch hitter needs the ability to sit on the bench for six or seven innings and then come into a game cold and get a hit, usually off one of the opposing team's best relief pitchers. It must be hard enough to hit a ninety-five-mile-an-hour fastball, but when you're in your midthirties and you've been drinking coffee on the bench the entire game, it becomes nearly impossible. Or at least that's what the Greg Norton experience has led us to believe.

I feel bad heaping too much blame directly onto Greg Norton. Going into the 2009 season, Norton was eleventh on the all-time list with 13 pinch-hit home runs. He probably didn't ask to repeatedly be placed in the most pressure-packed situations possible. Oh, and Norton did have a game-winning RBI against the Dodgers on August 1. Thing is, it was the only game-winning RBI he had all season, which was remarkable considering how often he got involved in games with a chance to directly alter the outcome.

While he may not have been much of a hitter, Norton was very good at working his plate appearances into walks; in 2009, he had almost twice as many walks (20) as hits (11). Norton's ability to draw walks, when contrasted against his inability to get important hits, suggested that he was past his physical prime. He was still mentally able to recognize pitches, and he knew when a pitch was heading outside the strike zone, but he wasn't able to react in time when one was coming into the zone. He knew when to swing and when not to swing, but recognition without reaction conspired to make Greg Norton a below-average baseball player.

In the midst of his epic struggle, Norton told Carroll Rogers of the *Atlanta Journal-Constitution*: "The disappointing thing—and I alluded to it earlier this year—the whole pinch-hitting thing isn't what your batting average is, which people seem to look at . . . It's how many big hits you have. I was in a situation last night where, going home, I felt like I lost the game."

Entire schools of thought developed as people tried to figure out what Bobby was doing using Norton so often. Facebook groups were organized, including two separate factions each named "Greg Norton Sucks," and Braves fans overloaded message boards venting their frustrations. Hey, I understood. I felt a certain degree of empathy for the man, but Greg Norton's job on the Braves made no sense in relation to his baseball skills. It was as if I had suddenly been asked to become a Victoria's Secret lingerie model. I would try my best, but I'm certain the people watching would be disappointed each time I strutted down the catwalk in a G-string-and-bra combo. I could try over and over, but the results would never change.

When I was sixteen years old, I was willing to do anything to make Coach B's junior varsity basketball team. I'd played basketball my entire life, and by the time I got to high school, I'd become an above-average player. I wasn't great, but I was playing year-round in church leagues, and my friends and I played every afternoon, pretty much seven days a week. I spent hours working on my jump shot in our driveway, learning the proper form from magazine articles and a used book about Larry Bird that I bought at a thrift store. (Key lesson: when lining up for a jump shot, the index finger *always* goes over the air valve.) I was good at organized basketball: I knew all the rules, I mastered the basic skills, I played with the confidence of someone who knew what he was doing. During elementary school, my final year of playing little league basketball on an eight-foot goal, I was the tallest and widest kid in the league, and my team won the championship game 31–27. I scored 29 of our 31 points, while one kid on the other team had 25 of the 27 for his team.

And yet I wasn't very good at "unorganized," or pickup, basketball. I'd started watching the Atlanta Hawks, specifically Dominique Wilkins, between Braves seasons, and I came to the alarming realization that the way I played basketball wasn't anything like National Basketball Association basketball. They played with anticipation and athleticism and style and verve, things I'd never even considered to be part of basketball success. So I began running up and down the court pigeon-toed, just like Dominique, hoping that would make me an ethereal dunker. It didn't, but my pediatrician decided that I had flat feet and needed to insert arches in my shoes. I didn't have the nerve to tell him that it was an entirely self-induced affliction.

After hooping in PE class and seeing the level of competition, I knew I wasn't good enough to make the middle school team. And I didn't. But I vowed to work harder and make the junior varsity team in ninth grade. I did not make the team, and I tried very hard to feel sorry for myself. Honestly, though, I should have been cut, because with my Pillsbury build and slothlike speed, I would have been no match for the rest of the team, even in practice. When you get cut from a team in high school, coaches love to talk about how Michael Jordan got cut from his high school team when he tried out as a ninth grader, which is true. But they always fail to mention that he was six four and could dunk at the time. I could barely pee in an adult urinal.

I played on four church league teams that winter, and my hormones finally complied with my will, shooting me up to five ten while leaving my baby fat behind. When hoops season rolled around that fall, only ten or eleven guys tried out for the JV team, so I knew that mathematically I had an excellent chance of making the team. By the third or fourth day of tryouts, only nine guys showed up, and it was seeming inevitable that I'd make the cut. The girls' varsity and junior varsity basketball teams were practicing in the school's main gym, and when they finished, the boy's varsity had dibs on the court. The gym the JV boys were assigned to use—dubbed the "old gym," because it had been the school's main gym in the 1940s before being repurposed as an auxiliary exercise room for PE classes—was in the midst of a renovation. As a result, the JV boys team had to resort to going to the outdoors cement courts behind the neighboring elementary school, where there was only one rim attached to a backboard, and the court was covered in leaves. Since it was early October, the weather was cool, and we would occasionally be forced to run through drills wearing jeans and long-sleeved shirts.

These workouts were supervised by Coach B, who taught physical education at a local elementary school during the day, and then in the afternoons coached all sorts of stuff at our high school: assistant football coach, JV basketball coach, varsity baseball head coach. He was about my size, with skin the color of cappuccino. He dressed like a coach: sneakers, sweatpants, golf shirts, a baseball cap tilted back at an angle atop his head. One day while we were running lay-up drills, Coach B made an offhand comment that he would "have a uniform for everyone here." I hid it, but I was elated: I had made the team. I had done it. Ten years of playing basketball every day had finally paid off in the spectacular prize of an ill-fitting polyester uniform.

I understood that I was overmatched, at least from an athletic standpoint: two or three guys on the team could dunk a basketball. But I knew the little things. I understood spacing, ball movement, defensive positioning, and I discovered on the fly that these skills had value regardless of my level of athletic ability. If I stuck to what I was good at, I would at least be able to compete.

Our opening game was at our archrival. All of us on the JV team wore our warm-ups to school that day, ostensibly to generate awareness and school spirit, but, really, I wore mine because I wanted everyone else to know that I was on the JV basketball team. Finally, I had a verifiable identity: I was an Athlete. While that designation may have been unofficial or self-supplied in the past, this crappy warm-up suit provided confirmation from an outside source for everyone to see.

We lost our opening game by 8 or 9 points, but I finished

with 4 points, 4 assists, and no turnovers, a stat line that amazed even me. The next day at practice, Coach B singled me out as one of the guys who had played well. And I *had* played well, turning in about thirteen minutes of mistake-free ball. I had been nervous and expected the worst, but somehow I got the best, or at least something about as good as my best.

It may surprise you to learn that not all fans of the Atlanta Braves are also fans of Bobby Cox. If this were a Venn diagram, I think there would be significant overlap, though not complete. And I'd estimate that the majority of the people who don't approve of Bobby do so passively—they believe that considering the rosters the Braves have assembled, the Braves should have won more games, should have had more success in the postseason, and they believe that Bobby should be assigned more culpability in the Braves' failure to do these things. But for the most part they swallow their criticism.

It's easy to blame players for their failure, but the baseball manager's primary job is to juggle the players so that they are on the field when they have the best chance to succeed. Bobby hasn't always done this. I'm not suggesting that he was involved in some nefarious plot to screw things up, but stuff just happens sometimes. Managers do their best to give their teams the best chances to win; sometimes things just don't work out, and sometimes managers must think long term versus short term. If you belong to this camp of Braves fans, it means that you believe that while Bobby should receive some blame, the Braves' failures are not completely his fault.

And then there are those people who think that Bobby

should receive every single bit of the blame. There are Braves fans out there who don't understand how Bobby Cox has kept his job this long, who think that fourteen division titles, nine trips to the National League Championships, five trips to the World Series, and one World Series win are the *minimum* of what should have been accomplished. With as much talent as General Manager John Schuerholz assembled from 1990 through 2007, and then Frank Wren through 2010, the argument goes, anyone could have accomplished what Bobby Cox accomplished. A *real* manager would've been able to win more than one World Series during that time span. Wouldn't he?

To which I answer: I don't know. As a general rule, but especially with sports, I find that arguing about the past is a pointless pursuit. What's done is done, and wondering what might have been generally serves only to cause frustration. I get the allure, though. One has to wonder how things would've gone if veteran outfielder Lonnie Smith had run the bases perfectly in 1991, or what would've happened if umpire Eric Gregg actually knew what a strike zone was supposed to be back in 1997. I just can't bring myself to do it. Or maybe I don't *let* myself do it.

Whenever I find myself defending Bobby Cox, I usually have to address his mismanaging lineups. And some of the things that Bobby does, I have a hard time defending. Like the whole Norton conundrum. While other hitters sat on the bench throughout Greg Norton's 2009 season, Bobby continued to run him up there. The unanswerable question was, Why? Why did Greg Norton receive chance after chance to hit with the game on the line? I don't want to make excuses for Cox: he had access to Norton's stats; he had the best seat in the house to watch him time and again. And certainly somewhere deep inside, at least one time during the 2009 season, I believe Bobby must have experienced that same nervous feeling Braves fans shared whenever Norton strode to the plate.

If he did feel that way, however, somehow Bobby is able to suppress it. For almost his entire tenure, he's had below-average guys playing important roles. Many have been catchers. This is partly Bobby's fault for using them over and over even as their stats plummeted, partly management's fault for not giving Bobby better parts to work with, and partly (and weirdly) Greg Maddux's fault. Throughout his time with the Braves, Maddux always asked for his own exclusive catcher, which basically meant that whoever the starting catcher was—the best catcher on the roster—wasn't the catcher on the days Maddux started.

Maddux's guys were generally referred to as his "personal" catchers. It made a certain amount of sense to give the starting catcher a day off every fifth day, since they tend to take more abuse than any other position player. And if you were going to have a below-average player in your starting lineup, who better to have him teamed up with than the greatest starting pitcher in the majors? Maddux could pitch with Bozo the Clown behind the plate and finish with five strikeouts and seven shutout innings.

A story in *ESPN the Magazine* suggested that Maddux liked pitching to catchers who could think "fast enough" to keep up with him, which, if true, means that Lopez's 214 home runs, 692 RBIs, and .286 batting average over the decade he and Maddux were teammates must have made him a slow thinker. I always believed that Maddux just wanted a catcher with whom he could spend more time going over strategy. While the starting catcher split his time with the other four starters, Maddux and his guy both had four days off between starts to sharpen their routines. And Bobby obviously didn't mind.

The only problem was that the Braves' backup catchers were profoundly challenged offensively. As Maddux's catcher, Charlie O'Brien batted .234, Eddie Perez batted .258, Paul Bako hit at a .205 rate, and Henry Blanco hit .202.

My JV basketball career was proving to me that, at least in Braves terms, I was probably more suited to be a backup catcher than a starting catcher. I had moved into the starting lineup as our shooting guard. I was averaging about 6 or 7 points, though we hadn't won a game. My role was to play the best defense I could, pass the ball to the open man, and shoot only if I was wide open and everyone else on the court had fallen over with severe cramps. Our showpiece that season was turning out to be a hulking freshman center, who wasn't exactly your classic low-post power player, though he had a great turnaround jumper that was close to unstoppable. He also possessed a volatile temper.

Our big problem was that we couldn't get a win. After an 0–4 start, Coach B juggled the lineup and inserted a kid named John at point guard. John had played some pickup ball and was very athletic, much more so than me, but he was very raw as a basketball player. He also kept to himself a lot, which didn't really win him any points with the rest of us. In his first start, John had a particularly brutal half, with five or six turnovers. John had a lot of confidence, and his playing style seemed to be completely derivative of popular NBA players at the time; he spent entire games trying to mimic the signature moves of

Michael Jordan and Magic Johnson. That John was fourteen years old at the time probably explained why he wasn't able to successfully replicate any of these moves. He didn't seem to grasp that by simply focusing on basketball fundamentals, he'd be a better player and make us a better basketball team. While he was slowly learning this lesson, the rest of us were watching our opponent run away with the game.

We went into the locker room at halftime down a dozen points. As we toweled off and gulped down Gatorade, we all found seats in the folding metal chairs and waited for Coach B to come in and critique us. He was a gentle man, so when the door exploded open and Coach B came rampaging through, everyone froze. He was one of the few black men I've ever known with green eyes, and when he was angry, it gave the unsettling effect that his eyes were on fire. This was one of those moments. He snatched a piece of chalk from the dusty tray under the blackboard and wrote "Turnovers 20" in angry block letters. He paused for dramatic effect and turned to look at us, then wheeled back around and scrawled "John 11" just underneath. We all looked at John, and he stared at the floor as though he was hoping a sinkhole would open right there and swallow him. To underline that we were turning the ball over too often, Coach B slapped the blackboard with an open hand, generating a loud *smack!* that genuinely surprised everyone. Coach's hard hit unintentionally dislodged a plaque hanging above the blackboard, and it flew off the wall and landed directly on Coach's shoulder. He tried not to show that he was in pain, though he obviously was. I nearly bit through my tongue trying not to laugh.

We bumbled to an 0–9 start, which was frustrating but not

really debilitating. If we continued losing each game by a close margin, it probably would have been much worse. But we were losing every game badly, by at least double-digits. Like Bobby Cox, Coach B was playing the players he had been given to work with. Also like Bobby, Coach B occasionally employed some strategies that might not have maximized the available talent. For instance, our glaring weakness was our inability to score points, which could be blamed directly on our "motion" offense, a very strict, pick-based offense that requires perfect execution, patience, and timing, much like the offensive set that the Princeton University Tigers are famous for using. We spent hour upon hour practicing motion, but it never helped. It was like asking a bunch of teenagers to work a nuclear fission assembly line; motion had so many complex, nuanced components that we were never able to make it work. Still, for whatever reason, Coach B insisted on sticking with the offense, and none of us dared to suggest that he rethink his coaching philosophy.

Our tenth game of the season was at a basketball powerhouse on the east side of town, a school with one of those gyms that was built in the 1960s in such a way that it will *always* look like it was built in the 1960s. We won the opening tip, and as we trudged into our motion offense, I threw the ball down to our freshman center in the post, who dribbled once and promptly had the ball stolen. He raced back, and around half-court he caught up to the guy who had stolen the ball. Instead of trying to poke the ball out from behind, he calmly and inexplicably reached out and swept the kid's legs out from under him. The poor dude went sprawling face-first into the floor, and our best player was immediately ejected from the game.

Without him, we stood even less than no chance to win, and

Coach B's season of frustration reached another boiling point. We were getting murdered in the middle of the third quarter when he called a time-out. He gathered us and calmly ordered us not to shoot the ball again. No one said a word. How do you respond to a command like that? We all grabbed our shorts and stood around waiting for the action to resume. Coach seemed as if he wanted to get on the bus right then. I was in the game at the time, so I was in the inner circle of the huddle, and after thirty seconds, nobody else had spoken. The buzzer sounded, demanding our presence back on the court, and all of us glanced around uneasily at one another. Were we really supposed to *not shoot* for the final ten minutes of the game? Finally, I turned to Coach B and asked, "So . . . what do you want us to do, then?" He looked me in the eyes and didn't say a word. He must have stared me down for ten seconds, which felt like ten thousand. I tried looking at the scoreboard, as if it would flash me some divine advice for dealing with Coach B. Finally, he turned and sat down on the bench without saying anything else.

Nobody was sure exactly what to do, but I was certain of one thing: I wasn't going to shoot the ball. We ambled back onto the court, inbounded the ball, and sheepishly went into our tragic motion offense. Unbelievably, after passing the ball around for nearly thirty-five seconds, the offense finally worked: I spotted a kid named Fred wide open under the basket. Fred was a JV football star who was a good enough athlete to be able to contribute on the basketball court, and he'd received sporadic playing time that season. I zipped the ball to Fred, and he sank a wide-open layup. Considering it was 2 of the only 20 or so points we'd scored up until then, I hoped Coach would be thrilled. As we sprinted back down on defense, out of the corner of my eye I saw Coach B stand up, stalk down the bench, and yank somebody by his warm-ups. At the next dead ball, Fred was substituted out of the game. We ended up losing 80–27, and we finished the season with a robust 0–12 record.

After our final game, I made a point of sidling up to Coach B on the bus ride home and thanking him for giving me a chance to play that season. I was genuinely grateful. Sure, we'd been terrible, but I'd been a starter on my high school's JV basketball team, which meant that Coach B thought I was one of the best basketball players in the ninth or tenth grades at our school. Whether I was or wasn't didn't actually matter. That Coach B had enough faith in me to put me out there on the court gave me a confidence in my ability to play basketball that I'd never had before.

Another recurring criticism of Bobby Cox related to his mismanagement of lineups is that he is too loyal to certain players. It's hard to argue that some players who probably shouldn't have been given opportunities were given opportunities, or that there have been situations over the last two decades where the player who was best suited for a situation was not the player Bobby deemed appropriate to use in that situation. Through the years, the Braves announcers—mostly Don Sutton and Joe Simpson—have wondered aloud if perhaps Bobby once had a manager who'd treated him poorly. As a reaction, they've posited, maybe Bobby goes out of his way to treat his players with loyalty and faith and respect.

I've often suspected the opposite: maybe Bobby once had a coach who trusted him and believed in him. Looking at Bobby's stats from when he played almost two major league seasons with the Yankees in 1968 and 1969, his batting average was bad (.225 career average), but he drew a lot of walks, giving him a .310 on-base percentage. He didn't hit for power, but the stats suggest he had a good eye. Actually, Bobby Cox's stats are pretty similar to those of a lot of the guys mentioned at the beginning of this chapter, the same guys we wonder why Bobby stuck by with such ferocity.

One recent weekday morning, as my wife and I were hurrying to get dressed and head out the door to work, Isabel asked me if I could walk our dog, Starbury. She normally handles the morning shift, I normally do the evening shift. I was running late also, but I agreed to swap spots in the rotation because Isabel seemed more harried than usual. Moments after she bustled out the door, I remembered that I had a meeting to get to, so I patted Starbury on the head and told her I'd walk her when I came home that night.

A couple of hours later, my wife called me at work and asked if I'd walked the dog. "Yes," I lied. I knew that if I was honest and said no, she'd harangue me about it for the next five minutes; saying yes seemed like the easiest way out, the path most likely to help me avoid immediate stress.

When I got home that night, Isa was already home. As soon as I walked in, I was hit with "Did you *really* walk Starbury this morning?"

I avoided giving a direct answer: "Why do you ask?"

Her suspicions were fueled by a few things: the leash being in the same place it had been when she'd left, Starbury's collar being in a different room than where we usually left it, and, most damning, a fresh pile of dog crap on the bathroom rug.

Though I'd spared myself five minutes of being yelled at earlier in the day, for the next six months or so, every time Isabel asked if I walked the dog, and I answered yes, it was followed by a withering cross-examination straight out of *A Few Good Men*. ("You want the poop? You can't *handle* the poop!")

I understood why Isabel couldn't have faith in me; I'd brought it upon myself. As Andre 3000 of OutKast once noted, "Faith is what you make it." Simply having faith in someone, whether that means trusting the veracity of his statements or his ability to succeed at a particular job, isn't enough to ensure his achievement in that situation. Whether or not he actually prevails in the moment is out of your hands, but at least he can't say you didn't give him every chance to make it big.

I've taken this to heart and try to give people the benefit of the doubt, because from what I've seen, I think Bobby Cox also understands the power of faith and what it means to have someone believe fully in you. Bobby doesn't seem to care what we, the fans, think about his managerial decisions, and he's never been the type of manager who felt compelled to explain his motivations to the media. He just wants his players to know that he thinks they're good enough to play for him; that he has faith in them. No matter what the fans are saying about them or angrily screaming at them.

CHAPTER 3

PERSISTENCE: How Mark Lemke Is Like Managing a High School Baseball Team

I played Little League baseball, but never with much gusto; basketball was my favorite sport. Like Kurtis Blow, I liked the way they dribbled up and down the court. Also, with basketball, I could practice it alone, whereas baseball required at least one other person to be a pitcher, catcher, or batter to approximate an authentic experience. The first year I played Little League baseball, my coach, a young guy named Stan, exhorted me to be more aggressive with everything I did on the field, not to be afraid to get in front of the baseball in order to knock it down and to hang in the batter's box against inside pitches. "Look," Stan leveled with me one evening after practice, his eyes darting back and forth as though he was about to reveal the ultimate secret to baseball. "The ball's not gonna kill you. It might hurt you pretty bad and it might be real painful, but it won't kill you. Probably not, anyway."

During my Little League career, after a brief stop in the outfield, I found a home at second base. According to Wikipedia, "the second baseman often possesses quick hands and feet, needs the ability to get rid of the ball quickly, and must be able to make the pivot on a double play."

Like most things on Wikipedia, this isn't completely true. We second basemen are historically little guys, the smallest players on the team. If we have quick hands and feet, it's probably because we've spent many years in school and around the neighborhood running for our lives to avoid conflict. Second basemen are bulldogs, feisty wee runts who play with vinegar and bile and leave each game splattered with dirt stains; equipment managers hate second basemen because they have to spend extra time cleaning their uniforms. Being a Braves fan, when I initially think of second base, Marcus Giles, Mark Lemke, and Glenn Hubbard come to mind—short white men who were rarely aesthetically pleasing but usually got the job done.

In recent years, the position has been gentrified by bigger and better athletes. Call me old school, but I still want my second baseman jug eared, with a thick goatee or handlebar mustache or some iteration of poorly planned facial hair, and maybe a strand of tobacco spittle dangling from his lips. He should wear eye black in every game, even at night. A player like Billy Martin or Phil Garner or Davey Johnson.

If through some wonderful freak of nature I was pressed into service playing in a Major League Baseball game right at this moment, I'd be a second baseman, just like I was most of the time in high school. I used to think I was positioned at second for my defense or because of my coach's eagerness to exploit my vast baseball acumen, but I knew the truth: it was because I was a below-average baseball player. I could hit a little and could field most grounders, but my arm was weak and inaccurate. I was too slow to play anywhere I'd need to cover a lot of ground. I played some catcher, too, but base stealers would take advantage of the noodle I had for a throwing arm.

Even in my physical prime, I never looked like the type of athlete who appears in advertisements for weight loss supplements, unless it was in the "before" picture. I was able to play on the high school team, however, because this was baseball. Take one look at some of the Braves through the years—former closer Bob Wickman immediately comes to mind—and they instantly announce that physical conditioning and success in baseball are not mutually exclusive, regardless of position. Second base is probably the ultimate hiding place for a below-average baseball player. Left field may be the classic place to stash old, broken-down infielders, but some combination of arm strength and speed are still considered essential to the position. At second base, the longest throw you'll ever have to make is a relay from the outfield to home or third, though that rarely occurs; mostly you're making soft tosses to first and underhand flips to second. The ground balls you face are commonly slow rollers from jammed hitters. You can play up close or back deep if you want, even all the way back on the outfield grass, with little consequence. Double plays are called for from time to time, but turning one generally means just redirecting a throw from the shortstop to the first baseman. An overzealous base runner may try to upend you, but the unwritten "phantom tag" rule allows second basemen to skirt actually having to touch second base in order to avoid injury. Even attempts to field fly balls are protected half the time by the infield fly rule, an odd baseball law that somehow allows infielders to drop pop-ups without penalty. If you're on offense, getting to second base means you've done only half your job.

You'd think second would be a place where serious hitters would want to play, since they'd have more effort reserved to hone their craft. But no, we second basemen generally are stationed toward the end of the batting order, a conduit between the power hitters in the middle and a trip back to the contact hitters at the top of the order. Second basemen might hit for average, never for power. When we even scratch out a hit, that is.

I t was on one of those trips with my grandparents, somewhere out upon the open road when I was stowed in the back of the station wagon, that my grandmother asked what I wanted to be when I grew up. I was old enough that this wasn't considered a completely far-fetched question. I could still change my mind, obviously, but it was time to at least start thinking ahead realistically. I knew, for instance, that my previously considered line of work—becoming a cowboy—was growing less likely by the year.

"A baseball player," I announced confidently.

I'd watched the Braves for no more than a year, but I'd practiced baseball in my backyard diligently. My dad would pitch me tennis balls, throw me grounders, whatever I wanted to work on. I particularly enjoyed attempting to catch fly balls that were just beyond my reach—diving, jumping, whatever it took to make the catch. Doing that made me at least feel athletic, even if I really wasn't.

When I announced that I intended to play professional baseball for a living, a smile split my grandfather's face. Paw

Paw would've liked nothing more than for me to become a professional athlete. Years later, he often drove three hours over from Alabama to see my high school basketball and baseball games. At this time, I'd played only one season of Little League baseball, but I'd been relatively good. My first game, the coach substituted me into right field midway through, and a fly ball was immediately hit to me. I remember feeling my nerves bubble up as the ball soared through the air, but I managed to calm myself, run under the ball, and then let it plop into my glove. The crowd went wild; we were so young that the outfielders hardly ever caught fly balls. Kids were usually stationed in the outfield because they *couldn't* catch. With my one grab, I instantly became regarded as one of the best defensive players on the team.

Nana followed up her initial query with, "What position do you want to play?"

"Center field," I answered quickly. My favorite player on the Braves at the time was the outfielder Brett Butler, a fair-hitting, speedy, defense-first center fielder. When my little league coach had asked me which number I'd like to wear, I'd requested Butler's number 22. The coach told me that I had to pick a number between 1 and 14. I asked for 3, for Braves outfielder Dale Murphy, but that was taken. Instead I selected number 2, one-half of the digits Butler wore. It wasn't until later that I realized the number 2 might be mistaken as a show of support for reserve Braves outfielder Albert Hall, who wore number 2.

"Outfield," Nana said, more statement than question. "You have to be really fast to play in the outfield." Nana wasn't a die-hard sports fan, but she was a sharp woman, very aware of the world around her. I hadn't known her to be wrong about anything, ever. If she said speed was a necessity in a major league outfielder, I would take her word for it.

This immediately presented a problem. I could catch the ball almost every time it was hit to me. But I was slow, glacially slow. This isn't generally apparent in Little League baseball, because you play on a shrunken field; even a ball drilled into a gap only takes five or six steps for the outfielders to reach. Still, I knew I was slow just from playing around with my friends. When we sprinted around my friend Allen's backyard attempting to shoot each other with BB guns, I'd quickly and painfully notice I was the slowest in our group. And things didn't seem to be changing as I grew older.

This was the first time I'd had to confront the possibility that I might not go on to become a professional athlete. What would I do when I grew up? I had no idea.

By the time I was in eighth grade, my final year of middle school, I *knew* I wasn't going to be a professional athlete. There was still enjoyment to be found in playing sports, but I didn't cling to any delusions. In retrospect, it was good to have an early grasp on my limitations, which also definitely included algebra, a perfect storm of a subject I didn't care about and a teacher I didn't care for.

About a month into the school year, my friend Shuford and I, who were in algebra together, mentally checked out. It was obvious we could make passing grades without having to devote ourselves entirely to the class, and if we didn't have to, why bother? The teacher in the classroom next door to algebra was named Mr. Fletcher, and he taught advanced math and computer programming to the oldest kids in our school. He wore thick glasses, was obese, and had wild, wiry, graying hair. Most of the students just left him alone. Shuford somehow discovered that Mr. Fletcher was a sports fanatic, and the two of us began to talk to him from time to time about baseball, basketball, football. After a few weeks, Shuford and I started going to algebra for roll call, then leaving class and just hanging out in Mr. Fletcher's room throughout first period. He had first period as a planning period, so he had no students. We'd spend the hour trying to stump each other with sports trivia or playing stat-based computer sports simulations Mr. Fletcher had ordered from computer magazines. It was actually a lot of fun; probably the most fun I had in middle school. Also, I made a D in algebra.

Years later, the summer before my senior year in high school, the Atlanta public school system consolidated my high school with our nearby rival, and my senior class immediately went from having about 250 students to over 600. The plan was for everyone to eventually be at a new campus, but it would take awhile to build, so they jammed all of us into my school, which they supplemented with a series of haphazardly placed trailers. If you've ever been curious about what it would be like to go to school in a trailer park, I can tell you.

Besides combining the students from the two schools, they also merged the staffs and hired a few new teachers. To my surprise, one of the new teachers was Mr. Fletcher, who had undergone a radical makeover: his hair was shorn close; his glasses had been upgraded to a newer, more stylish model; and most shockingly, he'd dropped at least one hundred pounds and was now fit and trim.

Four years had passed since I'd last seen Mr. Fletcher, but, aside from his extreme appearance change, he'd remained the same stat-obsessed sports fan. Shuford and I quickly fell back into hanging out with him and discussing sports whenever we got the chance. Because it was my senior year and I'd completed most of my required classes, I managed to schedule back-to-back periods where I was to serve as an assistant in the main office each day. Nobody required my attendance—my main job seemed to be covering for secretaries who went to lunch—so I spent many days hiding out in Mr. Fletcher's room, running computer simulations of baseball or basketball.

My freshman year of high school, I'd played JV baseball. Sophomore year I played JV baseball and basketball. Junior year I played varsity basketball. Senior year, at a much bigger school and with a debilitating sense of ennui setting in as the year progressed, I decided to play basketball and nothing more. I knew I didn't have an athletic future after high school, and I was looking forward to having time that spring to do whatever it was that seniors did when the end of thirteen years of forced schooling was finally in sight. For most of my classmates, this meant ditching school early every day. For me it meant becoming . . . Bobby Cox?

Even though Marcus Giles played 141 games for the Braves in 2006 and finished the year batting a respectable .262, the Braves let him walk away when the season ended, after every team in Major League Baseball refused to give them anything of value in return for Giles. This caused something of an uproar among casual Braves fans, because Giles had been the starting second baseman for four years and hit over .300 in two of those seasons. Not insignificantly, he had worked his way up through the Atlanta minor league system after we'd selected him in the fifty-third round of the 1996 draft. He was one of ours, a player we'd plucked from obscurity and then developed into an all-star in 2003, and the Braves tossed him out, not even able to trade him for anyone worth having. Surely there was something or someone out there we could have received in return?

But some of us more fastidious Braves fans understood why Giles needed to be replaced. Although Giles's batting average was better than those of some of his recent teammates, he'd been asked by Bobby Cox to move from his customary second slot in the batting order, where he'd always been relatively productive, up into the leadoff position. The leadoff hitter is charged with getting on base in any possible fashion, from working a walk to throwing his triceps in front of an inside fastball. Instead, Giles seemed to approach every pitch as though hitting a home run was his solitary goal. So he repeatedly took huge, wild, uppercut swings at the ball, corkscrewing himself into the dirt whenever he missed.

When he connected perfectly he could hit the ball pretty far—Giles poked 21 home runs in 2003. But the Braves felt that connection wasn't happening often enough to justify the millions of dollars he was due according to MLB's sliding salary scale. I was initially leery of Giles leaving, mostly because the only second basemen with major league experience that the Braves had left were Chris Woodward and Pete Orr, both guys who were below-average hitters, even for second basemen, and were at best average fielders. But I was also tired of seeing Giles repeatedly either strike out or loft unthreatening fly balls to right field.

While Giles's numbers dipped atop the order, he didn't fall completely apart: While he batted .262 in 2006, his 11 home runs and 60 RBIs were still better than anything the Braves' regular second baseman in the nineties, Mark Lemke, ever posted.

So why would a baseball team let such a productive player, still in his prime at age twenty-eight, leave while getting nothing in return? Because Giles was the second baseman, and anyone can play second base. As if solely to prove my point, instead of signing a veteran free agent to play second, the Braves took a left fielder coming off major reconstructive surgery on his throwing elbow and stuck him at second base and in the leadoff slot. His name was Kelly Johnson, and he was known mostly for displaying a terrific eye at the plate. When he first came to the majors two years earlier and immediately endured a 1-for-30 slide, Cox stuck with him. What exactly was it that the manager saw in Johnson then, when Johnson couldn't get a hit to save his life, that made him believe Johnson could not only move to a position he'd never played before but also bat leadoff for a team expected to contend for a title?

Johnson began the 2007 season ice cold, hitting .150 through April 16. He then reversed it and went 22 for 46 over the last two weeks of April. Through the first half of the '07 season, Johnson batted .288. He had 8 home runs, 41 RBIs, and, most impressively, his on-base percentage was .388—for every ten times he came to the plate, he managed to get on base four times, a rate high enough to place Johnson ahead of superstars like Alex Rodriguez and Ryan Howard. But it wasn't good enough for him to keep his job: toward the end of the season, the Braves called up a highly rated rookie, shortstop Yunel Escobar, who they stuck at second base (because, again, anyone can play second base), and they asked Johnson to split his time with Escobar.

In 2008 the Braves traded away shortstop Edgar Renteria and slid Escobar over; Johnson was given back second base, and he had the best season of his career to that point, starting 135 games, hitting .287, and even putting together a 22-game hitting streak.

In 2009 Johnson started strong, then hit a slump, and the Braves put him on the disabled list with wrist tendonitis. They sent him to the minor leagues briefly, and in the meantime, longtime Atlanta minor leaguer Martin Prado found a groove and took Johnson's spot at second base. In the winter of 2009, the Braves ended up letting Johnson walk without getting anything in return, just like they had with Giles.

From 2001 through 2009, Marcus Giles and Kelly Johnson logged the majority of starts at second base for the Atlanta Braves. Both guys had solid careers as Braves, but to be fair, Giles and Johnson had a tough act to follow. Between 1990 and 1997, when the Braves were reeling off division titles and World Series appearances, Atlanta's second baseman was Mark Lemke. The native of Utica, New York, was an appropriately small man for second base—five ten on tiptoes, no more than 170 pounds—and a spark plug, tenacious, a grinder. With a wad of tobacco in his cheek, a gap between his teeth, a perpetual two days' worth of stubble on his face, and a uniform permanently streaked with mud, Lemke was so earthy that his teammates started calling him "Dirt." Now, this—*this*—was a second baseman.

Lemke managed to keep the starting second baseman job for eight seasons, even though he never hit higher than .294, never had more than 7 home runs in a season, never drove in more than 49 runs in any one year. (Inexplicably, he did hit

.417 with three triples during the 1991 World Series.) What Lemke excelled at was defense: From 1990 through 1996, Lemke's fielding percentage bettered the league average for second basemen.

What ended up being the downfall of both Giles and Johnson was that they couldn't sustain their production. They were all over the place from week to week, and even though, at their best, they were both well above average, at their lowest they weren't good enough. But Lemke was so steady, so solid. And in 1997, the moment the one thing he had going for him, his defense, finished exactly tied with the league fielding average— the moment that Lemke was no longer above average—the Braves let him go.

One day in the winter of my senior year, I was hanging out in Mr. Fletcher's classroom, debating whether the Braves would be able to repeat their recent surprise trip to the 1991 World Series against the Minnesota Twins, which Atlanta lost in the bottom of the tenth inning of a hard-fought game seven, 1–0. "By the way," he said, "I have a proposition for you. Have you ever managed a baseball team?"

The new school's athletic director had approached Mr. Fletcher and asked him if he'd be interested in coaching the JV baseball team. Mr. Fletcher loved the idea and seemed suited for it—he certainly knew more about baseball history than anyone I'd ever been around. There was, however, one major problem: as it turned out, Mr. Fletcher's body makeover had actually been a medically mandated larger lifestyle change. When he was heavier, he'd developed a terrible problem with stress and ulcers. He'd been able to regain some measure of control over his life by cutting back on his eating, exercising regularly, and, curiously, by refusing to make any decisions unless they were completely necessary. As unconventional as this sounds, this last part was apparently key to Mr. Fletcher's improved health. Because while he was very interested in coaching the JV baseball team and putting some of his accumulated baseball knowledge to practical use, he informed me that he wouldn't be able to make any decisions, for fear of triggering an ulcer attack.

And so Mr. Fletcher's proposal was this: he would contact the school's athletic director and agree to coach the JV baseball team. I would unofficially serve as his assistant coach, since students weren't allowed to coach high school teams. Mr. Fletcher would attend every practice and game, and he would freely offer advice on ways to improve our team. He would sit alongside me in the dugout, though he would only be able to sit there and squeeze a tennis ball, as it helped alleviate his stress. But any and all strategic decisions would be made by me, and I would have the final say on every decision. Mr. Fletcher's stomach wouldn't have it any other way.

I was in. I'd already spent years second-guessing Bobby Cox, and now I had an opportunity to prove to the dozens of people who would see the junior varsity baseball team play that even at just eighteen years of age, I was already capable of being a Major League Baseball manager. The job turned out to be not only fun, but it gave me the opportunity to spend each spring afternoon out in the sunshine and grass, playing in the dirt like a kid with these kids. I got to wear a whistle around my neck, and I tried hard to treat our players as valued assets rather than as worker drones. Just like Bobby Cox.

Mr. Fletcher and I really had only two above-average pitchers, though since we played just one game each week, we figured we could get by with just the two of them. Our best all-around player was our ninth-grade third baseman, a kid who'd obviously played baseball his entire life, could hit for power, and played good defense.

Other than that, our team was very inexperienced. Our school's campus was smack in the center of Buckhead, one of the most affluent, richest neighborhoods in all of Georgia. The Atlanta Public Schools had an arrangement by which it bused students from Atlanta's predominantly black neighborhoods into Atlanta's white neighborhoods to go to school. I know the legality of this has been debated for years both before and since, but I can tell you that it worked for me, exposing me to new cultures, kids with different socioeconomic backgrounds, and, most relevant to my future employment, it taught me about sports and hip-hop music.

Most of the kids who signed up for the JV baseball team were black kids who bused in each day and who had never played organized baseball. They had watched baseball on TV, and maybe they'd played Wiffle ball or even softball in PE, but very few of them had ever been on an actual baseball team. While they were athletic enough to be good baseball players, few of them owned gloves, and even fewer of them had cleats. They signed up to play because they wanted something to do after school, and they were willing to work hard and play hard.

Our biggest need was at catcher. I'd played catcher on and off since Little League, mostly as a backup, and I knew what to look for in a starting catcher. First and foremost, a catcher has to be able to catch the ball, which is harder than it sounds.

Catching a ball thrown across the infield or in from the outfield is one thing; catching a ball fired across the plate as hard as the pitcher can throw it, while you're squatting and wearing about ten pounds of equipment in the sticky, humid Georgia spring is something else. Only one of the kids who came out for the team had any experience catching, and he wasn't very good at it, to be honest.

To remedy this need, Mr. Fletcher and I decided to *make* a catcher. We had about six outfielders, all kids who were super-athletic but unnatural baseball players. We targeted a freshman named Hilton, who had a good arm, was on time to every practice, and seemed to be the most interested in improving as a baseball player. One day after practice, we asked Hilton to stay a few minutes. I asked him if he knew anything about catching; he didn't, but he was willing to give it a shot. The only real downside to this was that we'd have only two weeks to teach him everything we could about being a catcher. The upside was that he hadn't yet learned that being a catcher mostly sucked. As a ninth grader, I'd volunteered to catch for the JV team because I knew I'd get to play. I ended up splitting time between catching and playing second base, and the entire time I was playing catcher, I wondered why I'd ever volunteered to catch. My knees still regret that decision today whenever the weather changes. The most exciting part about it was calling the pitches, trying to outthink the hitters. However, even having that control of the game, at least for me, did not outweigh the drudgery involved.

I decided it was best not to tell Hilton about this part. I helped with all the equipment, showed him how to strap on the shin guards, how to keep the catcher's mask tight but not so tight that you couldn't yank it off. I showed Hilton how to wear a batting glove under the catcher's mitt to soften the blow of fastballs, how to fit a dish sponge in there if they were hurting too badly, advised him to squat rather than sit on his knees, as it would make chasing after wild pitchers easier. I showed him, if a ball was popped up nearby, how to fling his mask far away rather than dropping it, to avoid having to worry about tripping over it. Lastly, I assigned him homework: watch the Braves every night and try to figure out what Greg Olson was doing behind the plate. No kid hates being asked to watch TV for his homework.

To our surprise and delight, Hilton embraced playing catcher. His technique was sloppy, but he was agile and eager enough to make all the required plays. That he had a good arm was an added bonus; we would've used an armless man behind the plate as long as he could stop the ball somehow or another. What Hilton didn't grasp as quickly was the art of calling the pitches, so we left that to me. Before every pitch, Hilton would look to me over in the dugout, and I'd hold up one, two, or three fingers, which Hilton and I would designate before each inning as representing particular pitches.

Somehow we finished that season 8–0. Managing the team was surprisingly easy. More than anything, I tried to remain upbeat. I never criticized anyone in front of the team, never raised my voice at a player in anger, and tried to exude a confidence that everyone could feel. It was fun coaching the guys, way more fun than I expected it to be, but the thing I enjoyed the most was seeing Hilton transform into a real catcher. He came to practice early, stayed late, actually watched the Braves, and tried to learn the craft of catching. That work ethic, that dedication to improvement, that persistence, was all I could ask from my players.

To me, persistence refers to the quality of someone's effort rather than the actual rate of effort or success. In the baseball context, maybe it means improving your fielding or your hitting. When you're faced with a task, you repeatedly throw yourself at it, and hopefully you break it before it breaks you. To borrow a line from Ed Harris, portraying NASA flight director Gene Kranz in *Apollo 13,* you "work the problem." This is apparently particularly helpful advice when you're trying to massage a box of spare space command module parts into an air filter.

While Mark Lemke was indeed consistent, it was his persistence that made him indispensable to Bobby Cox and the Braves. Look at those batting averages he posted year after year: .234, .227, .252. But he tried and tried and tried and tried, which is all you can ask from anyone, especially an undersized middle infielder.

All Bobby wants is for his players to go hard. You loaf, you're coming out of the game. Persistence isn't always measurable, a thing that can be tracked by Bill James or some stat program on a computer. But it can be learned, even by those of us who've spent large chunks of our lives avoiding having to give that effort.

There's a strange duality to being a Braves fan: we all have to accept that our team over the last two decades will forever be known for being really good but will probably never be known as one of the truly great franchises. Shouldn't they be known as great? Nobody in any sport has ever done what they've done, winning fourteen division titles in a row. The Braves and Bobby Cox might not have figured out how to get over that final hump consistently, but damn if they didn't persistently try to do it, which in the end is all a fan can ask for.

You can run, but life persists. The only way around it is to go right through it.

CHAPTER 4

CONSISTENCY: How Chipper Jones
Is Like Going to College

It takes a special kind of person to embrace a name like "Chipper," which if used as a moniker can make any person sound like a Boy Scout or perhaps an excitable female senior citizen. Then again, maybe Chipper isn't all that bad. The South is, after all, filled with unconventional names. Growing up, I knew a kid named Arkeith and an adult named Rolly. My aunt once worked in an Alabama college registration office, and came across someone whose first name was the single letter *B* and middle name was the single letter *C*. (He caused a stir when he registered for school and wrote his name as "B only C only," which led people to briefly think his name was pronounced Bonely Conely.)

I don't remember anyone in Atlanta really even making much of an issue over our third baseman having an adjective for a name. But then, Chipper Jones has always been a perfect fit in Atlanta, the de facto captain of the Braves for the last fifteen years, the most literal extension of Bobby Cox on the field, and in many ways, almost the king of the South—a modern-day Rhett Butler of baseball. Chipper grew up in Florida, but he talked and acted as if he'd grown up in south Georgia in one of those towns with an old-school name like Cairo or Montezuma. I once heard Chipper describe a fly ball out by noting he'd made contact "as hard as the good Lord can let me hit a ball."

Chipper's personal life briefly made headlines in the late nineties, as he went through a very public divorce, but we really only cared about the baseball, anyway. He'd been our best offensive player for a while, but with so much dominant pitching every evening, Chipper's offense seemed almost ancillary. When you see greatness every day, it can quickly become everyday. You learn to suspect the amazing and expect the extraordinary. And then it all begins to blur together, until eventually you're left looking at a guy on the way down leaving behind a collage of elevated standards and eye-popping records. Chipper is still a member of the Braves as I write this in the summer of 2010, but his time appears to be winding down. Chipper is already the only switch-hitter in baseball history to have a career batting average of at least .300 with at least 400 home runs. He's also one of only two men in the history of baseball with a career batting average of at least .300, 400 homers, and at least ten trips to the postseason. The other is Babe Ruth. Chipper has hit more home runs than any Atlanta Brave, ever. (Hank Aaron hit many of his when the Braves belonged to Milwaukee.)

Chipper's first full season with the Braves was in 1995, the only year of the Bobby Cox era when they won the World Series. In 1999 Chipper came of age, batting .319 with 45 home runs, 110 RBIs (his fourth of eight consecutive seasons at 100 or more RBIs, from 1996 through 2003), 41 doubles, and 25 stolen bases. He was selected the National League Most Valuable Player. In 2008, at the age of thirty-six, Chipper led the major leagues with a gaudy .364 batting average.

There were two things that always impressed me most about Chipper Jones:

1. It's easy to forget that Chipper was the first overall pick in the June 1990 amateur draft. The baseball draft is, at best, an inexact science. In the 1989 draft, the first overall pick was pitcher Ben McDonald, who went on to have a career MLB record of 78–70. In 1991 the first overall selection was pitcher Brien Taylor, who never even made it to the major leagues. As good a player as Chipper became, his success was never guaranteed. Yet for some reason, Chipper was able to put it all together and fulfill all the potential we saw for him. (By the way, the name of the Braves' general manager at the time who made the call to select Chipper first overall? Bobby Cox.)

2. Chipper's dominance of the New York Mets has been legendary and fun to watch, particularly for a Braves fan living in Manhattan. He hit so well at Shea Stadium—a career .313 batting average—that he named his son Shea, which I contend is probably the ultimate screw-you act by any athlete to a rival franchise. "How much do I own your team? I named my child after your home!" Through the end of the 2010 season, Chipper was hitting a career .319 with 44 home runs and 138 RBIs against the Mets. He'd also been intentionally walked 21 times in 215 games, which means that about every 10 games, the Mets got so frustrated with their inability to solve Chipper that they figured, "Ah, for-

get it, let's just walk him." The Mets had sought refuge in a new ballpark, Citi Field, and demolished Shea Stadium. In a memorabilia auction before Shea was imploded, Chipper bought two seats from Shea to be placed in his son Shea's room.

Keeping Chipper healthy has seemed like an increasingly uphill battle. That he tore the anterior cruciate ligament in his knee in just his eighth major league game wasn't a great omen. After recovering from that injury, for many years Chipper was about as durable as they come; between 1996 and 2003, he never missed more than 9 games in a 162-game season. But since 2004, he's only played more than 137 games in a season once. During the 2008 season alone, Chipper was listed at various times with each of the following maladies: acute tendonitis in the right shoulder, stiff back, right knee strain, stomach virus, left hamstring strain, strained right quadriceps, left eye contusion, slight tear in the right quad, back spasms, right groin strain, and strained right quadriceps. And that was the season he batted .364.

If Chipper has had an Achilles' heel with Atlanta fans, it's been this tendency to miss games due to injury. I've never been able to bring myself to criticize Chipper for his health, or lack thereof. Chipper is basically my age, for goodness sakes. There are mornings I can barely get out of bed; I can't imagine trying to get a bat out in front of a ninety-five-mile-per-hour fastball, four or five times a game, 162 nights a year. If he can play, we can always use him. If he's hurt, I'm only pulling for him to get healthy. He's been the most important Brave almost since he first stepped onto the field.

While the Braves spent the mid-1990s repeatedly returning to the playoffs and repeatedly asserting their dominance, I spent the bulk of this time accomplishing mostly nothing. I lived briefly with my friends Mike and Chris, for a few months (in two stints) with my parents, at one point moved into an apartment with my friend Matt, then eventually moved into a place with Matt and Mike.

During these same years, most of my friends were finishing college, looking for footholds in careers that interested them. I was finishing college as well, but in a different sense: they were graduating, while I, after two years at the University of Georgia and then a few quarters at a community college just outside Atlanta, had put my formal education on hold.

As I mentioned earlier, my grandmother was a highly decorated teacher. My mother was so studious that she graduated from high school early as a member of the National Honor Society and graduated college before she was twenty-one. Yet I never identified myself as an exceptional student, and barely identified myself as a student at all. I enjoyed the social interaction of being in school, made a lot of friends that I still have today. When I was in a class that engaged me, I could appreciate it, even look forward to attending. But most of the time, especially in high school, I found myself bored. I hated being assigned homework solely to keep me busy. I never had the patience to learn at a pace that was dictated to me. In high school I would read the entire textbook in the weeks after a class began, figure out whatever it was the teachers wanted me to know, make good grades on the tests, make bad grades on the homework assignments (mostly incompletes), and manage to do just enough to get by. I graduated from high school with a middling 2.7 GPA, but much better standardized test scores, which got me into the University of Georgia and a couple of other schools. Perhaps I was lazy, as most of my teachers suggested. I preferred to conclude that I was just unmotivated, because that takes the blame off my shoulders, fairly or not. Truth is, I liked learning, and I still do. I just like learning at my own speed. To me, being in school felt like being handcuffed.

I persisted through high school hoping that I'd find college to be different. At the University of Georgia, I had several classes in auditoriums with hundreds of people as my classmates. Even though we met in smaller groups during the week with teachers' assistants, I couldn't connect and never felt engaged. I knew I enjoyed reading and writing, so why did I need to take a geology class or a statistics class? Even in my journalism classes, a subject I was truly interested in, I found it hard to tune in. After two years of college, I wasn't sure what I wanted to do next. I just knew I didn't want to be in school.

This wasn't UGA's fault. I have nothing but fond memories of Athens and the University of Georgia. Athens is about an hour's drive from Atlanta, and I'd often eschew the highway so I could take two-lane roads through small towns like Dacula and Winder and Statham, just to roll down my windows and smell the clean air and drive past the antique shops and fresh vegetable stands. I was in Athens when Sid Bream slid across the plate to score the winning run in the 1992 National League Championship Series, and I'll always remember seeing the streets of downtown Athens instantly flood with students screaming and swinging from the traffic lights. I didn't take advantage of the legendary Athens music scene as much as some of my friends did, but I loved being on my own and being responsible for myself. I still follow UGA sports—live and die with UGA football every fall weekend—and I try to get back to Athens once each fall to attend a game in person. Most mornings when I was in school, if I had a break between classes, I'd grab a Coke and a newspaper or magazine and find a secluded bench somewhere on the North Campus. There among the leafy trees and bushes, sitting alongside centuries-old buildings ringed with columns, I never felt more collegiate. Many afternoons I'd go down to the student bookstore and hang out by the newsstand, where I'd read everything I could get my hands on. I'd flip through *Vanity Fair, The New Yorker, Rolling Stone,* and *Esquire,* and would study the articles and think to myself, someday I'm going to write like this.

Looking back, I wonder if going to school is supposed to be about doing what you don't want to do. Maybe if I'd just stuck with it, continued grinding and working, I'd have stumbled out after four or five years with a degree for my wall, a notebook full of contacts, and a leg up on the competition. Maybe college would have taught me in four years what it otherwise took me ten years to learn about myself. The path I took to get to where I am today, while unconventional, was much tougher than it could have or probably should have been. Knowing what I know now, if I had to do it all over again, I like to think I would have worked my tail off in high school and college, and probably would have spent a couple of hours every night doing my homework instead of playing basketball at the student center or video games with my roommates or teaching myself how to play the guitar or reading books about HTML programming. I realize now that a college education has value.

But I also think developing your work ethic and drive is just as valuable.

After two years at UGA, I decided to regroup—like a meeting on the mound with Bobby in the middle of a particularly tough inning. Soon enough I was back in Atlanta in my parents' home, living in my old bedroom. My parents were probably concerned, though to their credit they allowed me to make my own choices. I was scared, honestly. I was right back where I'd started, with a vague idea of where I wanted to go, but no real clue of how to get there.

There was one saga a few years ago, during the 2007 season, when Chipper Jones and John Smoltz suddenly started letting each other have it, back and forth, via the media, over the course of several days. It was as if this had been building up for two decades, and then, with the Braves out of the playoff race for only the second time since 1990, and nothing else to do but wait for the season to end, they needed to vent. I honestly don't remember another intrateam feud over that time period, not one that lasted several days and certainly not one between the two most respected players on the team.

At the time, Chipper was battling a strained groin, exactly the type of nagging injury that has plagued him in the latter part of his career. After a loss that Smoltz started and Chipper sat out, the pitcher told the media, "You can't worry about who's in the lineup and who isn't. You can't worry about that stuff anymore . . . I certainly appreciate the effort of the guys who are on the field busting it."

This was interpreted as a shot at Chipper Jones. He hadn't

played, thus he wasn't on the field busting it. Smoltz appreciated the guys on the field busting it; so he didn't appreciate Chipper sitting out injured.

Chipper said he would try to play the rest of the games that season. To this, he added, "Somebody I know better not miss a start."

Back to Smoltz. He was asked if he had indeed been talking about Chipper. "I have no comment. I'm not even going to address that," Smoltz said, by way of addressing it.

When asked if he had spoken to Smoltz, Chipper said, "I got nothing to say. He made his point through the media. Now I'm going to make my point through the media. If he doesn't want to do it man to man, then fine."

Neither player was exactly Iron Man. In 2007, when the Smoltz/Jones cold war was under way, Chipper had already missed extended time after colliding with a runner while trying to field a grounder, and somehow—and this is something only Chipper Jones could do—he'd sprained both of his thumbs at the same time. Meanwhile, in the years before this disagreement, Smoltz had undergone four different surgeries to his pitching elbow; a year later he'd have surgery on his pitching shoulder.

This cosmic schism between Smoltz and Chipper endured for about three days, a long seventy-two hours that seemed to hold the future of Braves Nation in the balance. Was this it? Was this how it would all end? We had no idea how this would play out, and we watched for signs of resolution like the faithful waiting for the cardinals in the Vatican to elect a pope. Just as things reached a boiling point, Cox and Schuerholz finally issued a call for a sit-down with Jones and Smoltz.

I imagine their meeting went something like this:

FADE IN

INT MORNING: TURNER FIELD

MUSIC IN—"For What It's Worth" by Buffalo Springfield.

JOHN SCHUERHOLZ and BOBBY COX are walking together through a dark, dank, cement-floored hallway underneath Turner Field toward the Braves' locker room. The camera follows them in a long tracking shot, like the restaurant scene in Goodfellas. *They pass security guards and the occasional Braves player. SCHUERHOLZ is wearing slacks, a dress shirt, and a tie with matching suspenders. Every hair is in place, and he projects confidence. He wears a BlackBerry holster on the front of his waist and a Bluetooth earpiece in his ear. COX is wearing flip-flops, sanitary socks, stirrups, shorts, and an Atlanta Braves T-shirt and hat. A towel is draped around his neck. In his hand is a Gatorade cup filled with steaming coffee, black. COX looks a little crusty, as though he just woke up.*

They reach a door marked Locker Room. SCHUERHOLZ places his hand on the door handle and pauses. He turns to face COX, who looks to the side and unleashes a long stream of ebony tobacco spit. It splatters noisily onto the floor.

SCHUERHOLZ
Bobby, can you watch it? These are brand-new loafers I just got at Off Saks . . .

COX

(Grunts, still looking at the floor.) These are $3.99 flip-flops. I got them for free from the closet in the trainer's room.

SCHUERHOLZ

(Smiles.) Look, this . . . whatever you want to call it between Chipper and Smoltz . . . it's gone on long enough.

COX

I agree.

SCHUERHOLZ

The latent negative tension from this Smoltz and Chipper thing is threatening to derail not just this season but the entire clubhouse. It's not good, and worse, it reflects poorly on the both of us. If we don't . . .

COX

(Interrupting.) I'll handle this.

COX reaches over and pulls open the door.

INT: LOCKER ROOM

He walks over to the locker of JOHN SMOLTZ. SMOLTZ is sitting quietly in a leather office chair, dressed similarly to COX, in baseball's undressed uniform, counting out tickets, stuffing envelopes, and writing names on the outside. COX leans in closely.

COX

Smoltzy, need to see you in my office.

SMOLTZ doesn't look up, just sets down the stuff he's working on and follows COX across the room and toward his office. As they walk, SCHUERHOLZ falls in step with COX, and CHIPPER JONES sidles up alongside SMOLTZ.

FADE OUT: MUSIC

INT: COX'S OFFICE

COX enters and sits heavily at his desk, a cheap, battered metal table. SMOLTZ and JONES sit in the two folding chairs facing the desk. COX sets down his coffee cup and leans back in his chair. SCHUERHOLZ goes to a seat in the corner and cracks open a bottle of water.

COX

Chipper, I met you when you were still in high school. John, I've known you since you had hair. We've spent more time with each other than we have with our families, haven't we?

JONES AND SMOLTZ IN UNISON

Yes, sir.

COX

Okay, so listen: What have I been telling you guys for the last dozen years? Guys—and this goes for you, too, Schuerholz—there have been times over the last fifteen years when I've disagreed with every one of you.

FADE IN MUSIC "THE BATTLE HYMN OF THE REPUBLIC."

COX

Look, none of us are perfect. We've each our problems, each done things wrong.

SMOLTZ and JONES glance at each other briefly and then back at COX.

COX

In all that time I've known you boys, have you ever heard me say a bad word about either one of you to anyone? Ever? Chipper, do I say anything to the media when you strike out in the clutch?

JONES

No, sir.

COX

Smoltzy, do I say anything when you tell me your arm feels fine but I leave you in and you get rocked?

SMOLTZ

No, sir.

COX

Damn straight. We're a team, guys, a family. Every day, we show up and try as hard as we can, all of us. We're doing everything we can. Each time you swing the bat, Chipper, you're trying to improve on the previous swing. Johnny, every time you throw that slider, you're trying to make it more accurate, more nasty. You guys know that about each other, right? That you're both trying your hardest? That we're all trying our hardest?

SMOLTZ and JONES nod.

Let's squash this, then go out and play some baseball, the greatest game in the world.

JONES and SMOLTZ look at each other, pause, then shake hands.

COX

That's right, that's right. Make up. Now get out there and play ball.

FADE IN MUSIC "CENTERFIELD" BY JOHN FOGERTY.

SCENE FADES OUT.

Whatever happened behind that closed door, upon leaving the actual meeting, both Chipper and Smoltz were completely conciliatory.

Chipper announced: "Obviously, there was a misunderstanding. I apologized to [Smoltz] for my comments in yesterday's interviews. He assured me that he wasn't singling me out."

"It was a total miscommunication," said Smoltz. "It's over with and it won't be a problem the rest of the time that we're teammates."

Their answers may have sounded generic, but Smoltz was telling a truth: there was never a problem between Smoltz and Chipper again. Less than two years later, the Braves signed Chipper to a three-year contract extension worth $14 million a year. The Braves also offered Smoltz a new contract worth only about $2 million guaranteed. Smoltz opted for a contract with more guaranteed money from the Boston Red Sox, and like that, Smoltz was gone.

Chipper publicly expressed frustration and disappointment with the Braves losing a key pitcher and Atlanta icon, but out of all the original 1990s Braves, the franchise was now left in Chipper's hands alone.

Something had to give. After eating all of their food for a few months, I moved out of my parents' home and moved in with my friends Mike and Chris. I needed a job, and I had several, from working part-time at the church where I'd grown up, to working for my friend Bruce's consulting company building and designing these new-fangled things called web pages. I knew that at some point I'd have to find a career, but at the time, other than for rent and food, I didn't really have much need for money. I didn't drink or smoke or do drugs. I didn't have a girlfriend, and spent most of my free time playing basketball with Mike and Chris, so at least for a while, I could exist with only a part-time job. But I knew the clock was ticking, and eventually I'd have to find a career. I figured if I had to go back to college, I would, but I didn't want to. I'd flip through the classified ads in the papers and wouldn't see a lot of interesting jobs for people without college degrees. Or for writers.

I'd wake every day around 11:00 a.m. and work on whatever job I had at the time, then go back to my house around 5:00 p.m. and hang out with my roommates as they returned from full days of work or school. Then I'd stay up and watch sports on TV until two in the morning. Then I'd go to bed and read, though I didn't have a bedside lamp because I couldn't afford one and didn't want to ask my parents for one. Being resourceful, I used a flashlight I bought at a drug store. Then I'd fall asleep around 5:00 a.m. and do it all over again. Day after day.

My one respite was writing. Every day I'd script emails that were masterpieces. I'd write down notes about things my roommates said while watching TV. I'd write elaborate weekly recaps for the fantasy baseball league I was involved in. Fiction, poems, nonfiction, reporting, essays—I tried it all. I was realizing that I didn't so much want to write as I needed to write; it fulfilled some sort of gap in my soul. I didn't understand why I enjoyed writing, but I knew I wanted to get better at it, so I began to study it on my own, rereading my journalism and English textbooks, looking up tips and advice and famous articles on the newly sprouting internet. I spent a lot of time in my local library, checking out books about writing and writers, from Truman Capote to Gabriel García Márquez to George Plimpton to Gay Talese to William Shakespeare to Willie Morris to John Irving. These books became my college, the books themselves being the only loans involved. One night, I stumbled across a quote from Capote, who never attended college, that I allowed to spark hope in my heart: "I felt that either one was or wasn't a writer, and no combination of professors could influence the outcome. I still think I was correct, at least in my own case."

At the time, the internet was starting to bubble with content. I subscribed to an email newsletter featuring record reviews, and before long I'd emailed the editor asking for an opportunity to write for him. He started sending me CDs, and I emailed him reviews for free. I discovered a newly launched music website I enjoyed, emailed the editor, and got involved there, writing for free, doing reviews, and doing interviews with artists. (That site is actually still around and is now one of the most powerful music sites on the web—Pitchfork.com.) After a couple of years, I had enough quality clips under my belt that I felt confident enough to mail them out to the local papers with a query letter. Before long, against all odds, I was gainfully employed.

In everything I read, there was one theme I picked up over and over. To me, it was simple but profound: write. It's like hitting or pitching or any other skill. You can talk about writing, you can read about writing, but you have to write to get better at it. I wrote seven days a week, for a couple of hours a day, and this is something I try to adhere to today. If you want to improve at anything, you have to practice. Maybe I never put the requisite energy into school, but I've probably spent more time in my life writing than I've spent doing anything else. Oftentimes, sitting down to a blank screen or page, that cursor winking at me eternally and infernally, I still feel like a beginner, and I wonder to myself if I can move the words on my page around into such an order that they will resonate with someone else.

And then I hold down shift with my left pinky and try to figure out the future all over again.

What I most appreciate about writing is the same thing I came to respect about Chipper: it gives me a fidelity, a consistency. Like writing, Chipper was ever present in my life, there pretty much every day of the season via the magic of television or the internet.

Consistency is how we reinforce the things that are important to us. We want things we can count on, friends who put as much into a friendship as they take from it. Like being a friend, being a fan requires a similar give and take. You pledge yourself to a player, and all you ask is that he gives it his all every game. That's all Bobby asks from his players. That's all I ask from the Braves.

Each season between 2004 and 2008, Chipper managed to raise his batting average, from .248 in '04 up to that astronomical .364 in '08. And then in the 2009 season, Chipper's batting average slipped to .272 with a few weeks left. More alarming, his home run output took a nosedive, with only 16 at that same point in the year. During a late-season Sunday night game, an ESPN announcer wondered aloud whether we were seeing the final decline of Chipper Jones. I found myself afraid to consider this possibility.

Through everything, Chipper's consistency has been remarkable. Against right-handed pitching, his career batting average was .310; against left-handed pitching, .308. No major league player has played as long for only one manager as Chipper Jones has for Bobby Cox. That's in more than a century of baseball history. It is only through consistency that Chipper was able to become what he became, and that is the greatest representation of a city that an athlete can be. If Joe Namath will always stand for New York City and Magic Johnson will always be identified with Los Angeles, Chipper Jones is and will forever be Atlanta. For fifteen years (minus a couple of seasons in left field), Chipper has been snagging dribbling grounders to third with his bare hand, rounding first with his shoulders slightly twisted toward home, always there for us.

This is a tremendous part of the legacy of Bobby Cox. While Bobby certainly seems to prefer to err on the side of caution with any injury, he's also taught me the importance of giving effort in everything I do. A baseball season is an inordinately long time, from March until October, and a team might have, at most, three or four days off in a month. Think of how many mornings you must wake up and think, "This again?" But you do it, you just do it, over and over again, trying to get better at it each time.

That's what Chipper and Bobby have done.

And that's what I will continue to do.

CHAPTER 5

FAILURE: How David Justice Is Like Starring in a Commercial for a Gas Station

During his time with the Braves, from 1989 to 1996, David Justice compiled 522 RBIs, 160 home runs, and batted .275 with an .873 OPS (a stat combining on-base percentage and slugging percentage). He finished third in the MVP voting once, was a two-time all-star, and, arguably, in the 1995 World Series, hit the most meaningful home run in Atlanta baseball history. David Justice could have gone down in history as the greatest Brave of the Bobby Cox era.

But with David Justice, at least while he was a Brave, it seemed like it was never about what happened on the field. Today, of the first nine images that come up in a Google image search for "David Justice," five of the pictures feature him alongside the movie star Halle Berry, and one of those is a photo entirely devoid of David Justice. It shows Halle Berry alone from a movie, which in many ways is fitting. David Justice's best years in Atlanta will forever be entwined with Halle Berry.

David Justice's name made him sound like a superhero,

or maybe a backpack rapper. With a propensity toward jewelry that would've made Mr. T blush, not to mention a robust blast of self-confidence (as a young player, Justice drove a Mercedes with Sweet Swing vanity plates), Justice never lacked for swagger. He was the only Brave who regularly participated in MTV's Rock 'N Jock games (coincidentally, alongside future Braves pitching coach Roger McDowell), which is actually where Halle Berry first became familiar with Justice. While a lot of Braves players in the early nineties came from rural, proletarian backgrounds, Justice at the very least projected the image that he was big time, a guy born on Planet Hollywood for whom playing baseball in Atlanta was just a pit stop along the way to some undefined future bigger and better than anything Atlanta could offer. If the early nineties Braves were a movie, Justice would be the hot-shot kid who doesn't listen to anyone, the kind of character who wears sunglasses indoors and his hat backward who the manager just can't seem to reach.

Nobody ever questioned Justice's on-field production or talent—he was skilled enough to be unanimously considered one of the best players in baseball. Justice's first season in Atlanta was 1990, when he split time between first base and right field because he was stuck behind a veteran at each position: Braves legend Dale Murphy was in right; Atlanta would trade him later in the season. In the meantime, Justice ended up playing a lot of first base after Nick Esasky, upon whom the Braves had lavished a then extravagant contract worth just under $2 million a year, came down with, of all things, vertigo. After signing that three-year contract, Esasky played just nine games for the Braves before retiring. Justice cracked the lineup, batted .282 with 18 HR and 78 RBIs, and was named Rookie of the Year in

1990, which you might think would lead to a certain modicum of popularity. And I suppose it did. Still, only two years later, an Atlanta radio station had rewritten John Lennon's "Imagine," changing the verse to say, "Imagine no Dave Justice, it's easy if you try."

It seemed like there was always something happening with Justice. At the end of the 1991 season, when the Braves were finishing going from worst to first and could seemingly do nothing wrong in the eyes of Atlantans, Justice went out for an evening with fellow Braves rookies Brian Hunter and Keith Mitchell. The night ended with Justice home asleep, and Hunter and Mitchell each in separate single-car accidents and charged with DUIs. "You would rather not have this happen," John Schuerholz told the *Atlanta Journal-Constitution*. While Justice technically did nothing wrong, he was still in the middle of the situation.

A few months later, during spring training in 1992, wanting a new contract, Justice refused to pose for photos in his Braves uniform. Soon after getting a raise, he was quoted by a local newspaper reporter as saying, "There are a lot of good guys on this team, but there are a few who I know use the N-word when I'm not around." Later, Justice told the *Atlanta Journal-Constitution* that he'd been misquoted: "I expected [the writer] to write it exactly the way I said it, not to take bits and pieces . . . I would never say anything like that about my team." The writer in question, Bill Zack, said he had not only shown the article to Justice before publication but had discussed it with Justice after the story came out, and Justice had confirmed that the quote was correct.

Even though he projected a mostly bedazzled image, in reality Justice was just as blue-collar as anyone else on the Braves.

He grew up in a single-parent home in Cincinnati, raised by his mother. He went to an accelerated high school where he excelled academically and was able to skip seventh and eighth grades. He went to Thomas More College in Kentucky on a basketball scholarship, and it was there that he discovered baseball and, in turn, his future. It was never presented as an excuse, but perhaps immaturity played a part in Justice's early mishaps. He said things that nobody says to the media, because most guys understand that honesty almost always brings problems. As a sportswriter who is constantly interviewing athletes for a living, even I understand why some guys are less than honest about how they really feel. If they do say anything remotely controversial, it causes a media feeding frenzy, and everyone attacks to get their pound of flesh.

It's entirely possible that David Justice was too real for Atlanta. As I've observed traveling around the country, life in the South is different from life in other places. As a general rule on Southern living, sensitivity and civility usually take precedence over honesty and directness. This might not lead to the most open relationships between casual acquaintances and neighbors, but it works pretty well as a form of keeping a consistent if sometimes inauthentic peace. A lot of my friends and I were raised to say "please" and "thank you," to always suffix "yes" and "no" with "sir" and "ma'am." Things are slowly changing now, and it's not like I grew up in Elizabethan England, but even twenty years ago, there was a stricter code of civility in place. Being provocative for the sake of being provocative might be great shtick on talk radio and political television, but it didn't get you very far in some Atlanta circles.

I n the fall of 1998, my friend Andy called one afternoon to see if I'd be available to star in a television commercial. More specifically, Andy wondered if I'd be interested in being an extra in a baseball-themed commercial shoot for Speedway, a chain of convenience stores spread across the South.

Andy owned a retro sports apparel store that was located right in the middle of Buckhead, Atlanta's upscale nightlife district. I'd stumbled upon his store one day, written an article about it in Atlanta's weekly newspaper, and later become good friends with Andy and his co-owner, Bill. I spent hours at the store each week getting into misadventures, arguing about Bobby Cox's latest decision, talking about women and movies—basically, just being a guy. Being a freelance writer is a mostly solitary pursuit, with many hours spent alone, trying to figure out which words sound best in which order. Andy and Bill became the older brothers I never had. Because their store was right in the middle of Buckhead and open late on the weekend, Andy and Bill seemed to know many people who had plenty of free time on their hands: bartenders, the self-employed, writers. The ad agency working on this commercial offered each of us an outrageous amount, something like $500 cash, to come out for six hours and perform in this commercial. It would be euphemistic to describe my schedule at the time as "flexible." I was definitely in.

A few weeks before the shoot, I was hanging out at Andy's store one afternoon when we starting breaking down the casting of the commercial. We would need actors to portray a pitcher, a catcher, an umpire, a batter, a first baseman, a base runner, and an outfielder. I was hoping to get cast as the catcher, since I'd caught some in high school and was familiar with how to move and look like a catcher. But Andy had already promised the catcher role to someone else, so he suggested that I be the pitcher. I agreed to give it a shot. This pitcher was definitely one of the starring roles in the commercial, as it were, and I figured as long as I was going to appear in an ad for a convenience store, I might as well take the lead.

If we had been playing an actual baseball game, I would've been the worst possible choice to pitch—I have never been able to throw a baseball very fast, and I don't exactly have pinpoint control. But this wasn't a real game. This was a commercial, this was Hollywood, or at least what passed for Hollywood in Atlanta's burgeoning suburbs. I'd played and watched enough baseball to mimic the motion of a pitcher, and I knew that at the very least I'd be able to throw the ball close enough to home plate for a batter to make contact. According to Andy, even that much wouldn't be necessary—he assured me that since this was a commercial, all I'd have to do was give the *impression* that I was a pitcher, and then the editors and directors and whoever else would take care of the rest. Andy was making this thing sound like a James Cameron production. In retrospect, I suppose it should've raised a red flag that the casting director had apparently turned his or her entire job over to the owner of a store that sold throwback jerseys.

A few days later, a half dozen of us met up at a local high school field to pretend to be Major League Baseball players for a day. Driving up, I was shocked: This *was* a huge shoot, with wardrobe trailers set up, cameras mounted on cranes, even a craft services truck. Upon arrival, we were gathered together and briefed on the plot by an assistant director. Because it was going to be shot in a series of close-ups, there was very little actual action required. The commercial would open with a close-up of first base, where a runner would be taking his lead while the first baseman stood close to the bag. Cut to a shot of the pitcher as seen from the third base side of the field, where the runner could be seen lengthening his lead off first in the background. Cut to a traditional shot from center field, and the pitcher would deliver the pitch to home, where a batter would make solid contact on an obvious fly ball. Lastly, we'd see an outfielder jump in vain as the ball sailed over his glove and over the wall for a home run. These were the four shots we needed to film on this day. Then—and this was really the key part of the commercial; a shot that would be filmed some other time and place—the ball would land in the middle of a Speedway convenience store, presumably not maiming any shoppers on the way down.

Later they would edit in crowd shots and sound effects and somehow make it seem as though we were playing a highly important game of consequence in a major league stadium instead of on an empty high school field. I believe the ball crashing into the store was supposed to somehow be a metaphor for the quality of this convenience store chain, as though buying your soft drinks and gasoline at this establishment was a home run. A two-run home run, no less; why they didn't make it a grand slam was beyond me. Actually, the whole conceit of the commercial doesn't make any more sense to me now than it did then.

But I needed the money, so I showed up and shut up.

Halle Berry and David Justice married on New Year's Day 1993, about three months after the Braves lost their second consecutive World Series, and for the next few years, they were Atlanta's royal couple. We can only assume that being married to Halle Berry, at least during the newlywed stage of their relationship, must have been an endlessly inspirational experience for Justice. That first season after he put a ring on it, Justice posted incredible numbers: 40 HR, 120 RBIs, and 78 BB. A story in *Sports Illustrated* made their relationship out to be one ordained by fate. They each spoke to the writer as though they had finally found true love, and Justice attributed what was reported as a marked change in his attitude largely to Berry.

Justice and Berry became the toast of Atlanta, the Braves gave Justice a huge contract extension, and he was a key cog on their 1995 team that went to the World Series. During that 1995 World Series, the Braves had taken a 3–2 lead against the Indians when the series shifted back to Atlanta. Before game six, Justice was asked about the Atlanta fans, and he was quoted as saying, "If we don't win, they'll probably burn our houses down. If we get down 1–0, they'll probably boo us out of the stadium. You would have to do something great to get them out of their seats.

This caused an immediate storm. There was probably some truth to Justice's statements. He wasn't completely correct, but we Braves fans *were* frustrated. We knew the Braves were good, and we'd heard over and over again from national pundits that the Braves should win a championship. We suspected they were good enough to win one. But they just hadn't pulled it together. As frustrating as this must have been for the actual players on the team, for us as fans it was even worse, the flames fanned by talk radio and chatter among friends. A hint of desperation was setting in. We knew no dynasty could last forever. Could this one win the ultimate award before it was too late?

When game six started, David Justice was booed loudly and lustily. If Braves fans didn't actually want to burn his house down before the game, they sounded ready to do so now. It's hard to imagine how David Justice's time in Atlanta would have turned out if he hadn't done what he did next. But it did happen, and it changed everything, then and now and forever.

In the bottom of the sixth inning, with the game still scoreless, Justice led off the inning with a blast into the right field stands off Indians starter Jim Poole. Tom Glavine and Mark Wohlers combined to hold the Indians to only one hit over the nine innings, and it was over. The Braves won game six 1–0, and they—we—had finally won a World Series. "The fans were the biggest factor," Justice said after turning our boos into raucous cheers. "They proved me wrong. They definitely proved me wrong."

More important, David Justice proved us wrong. If we learned anything from David Justice, it was that production cures everything, even if only temporarily. After that hit, Justice could have owned Atlanta for the rest of his life. A couple of months later, just as the Braves started 1996 spring training in West Palm Beach, Halle Berry released a statement saying that she and Justice had been separated for some time and were going ahead with a divorce. A month and a half later, in the second inning of the Braves 40th game of the season, Justice swung at a pitch from Pirates starter Denny Neagle and dislocated his shoulder. He would never play another game for Atlanta.

Before the 1997 season started, the Braves traded Justice and center fielder Marquis Grissom to the Indians for fleet outfielder Kenny Lofton and reliever Alan Embree. At the time, the move was widely seen as a salary dump, as the trade committed the Braves to less money long term, and it opened up more playing time for a kid named Andruw Jones. Justice returned from his injury in Cleveland and helped the Indians to the World Series. The Braves kept right on rolling along without Justice, and they might have met Cleveland in the '97 World Series if it wasn't for Eric Gregg's ridiculous interpretation of the strike zone in the National League Championship Series.

Nobody wanted to dislike David Justice. He arrived in Atlanta with an empty slate, as capable of becoming a fan favorite as he was of being disliked. He wasn't totally unpopular—plenty of people were upset when he was traded away—and just recently he was inducted into the Braves Hall of Fame. Yet in retrospect, even producing the greatest moment in Braves history wasn't enough to save him, at least in that moment of his departure. Trading David Justice saved money, but more important, it cleared the air. Maybe the Braves thought that even though Justice was directly responsible for that title, they'd have to move DJ in order for the Braves to move on. It didn't work. Justice went on to play nearly 800 more games, hit 145 homers, and drive in 495 runs. Justice won another title, in 2000 with the Yankees, but that one World Series in 1995 was the only one the Braves managed. Fourteen division titles, one World Series win. Thanks to David Justice.

Justice could have struck out in every at bat in his Braves career other than that game six home run in the 1995 Series, and I would still be reluctant to characterize his career in Atlanta as a failure. He played just over 800 games with the Braves, more than Terry Pendleton, and yet Pendleton will probably always be remembered more fondly. If anything, David Justice represented a failure of our ability as fans to regulate our own hopes. After he won Rookie of the Year in '90, we projected David Justice to be the next Dale Murphy, the man he replaced in right field. Justice won us the ultimate prize, and he had a long and fruitful baseball career. It just didn't work out the way we Braves fans wanted it to.

B ill, Andy's affable co-owner at the store, was selected to be the celluloid batter who would hit the home run off me. With Bill and me in key roles, neither of us exactly physical specimens, this commercial was shaping up to look more like a men's slow-pitch softball game than a professional baseball contest.

A light rain started to fall as we began filming. The director was a man with long hair and sunglasses. He was wearing one of those safari vests that actors wear when they're portraying directors, and he told us we'd begin with the shot of the runner leading off first base. I can't remember who played the runner, but the first baseman was played by one of Bill and Andy's part-time employees, a guy named Don.

After a half hour of moving the cameras around and checking that the lighting was correct, we were ready for the first shot. Don went over to first and pretended to hold the runner on base, as whomever it was who played the runner carefully stepped off his lead. The assistant director yelled, "Action!" Don and the runner stood there for two or three seconds, crouching in place. The assistant director yelled, "Cut!" And then we broke for lunch.

As we sat around waiting to get back to work, an anxious feeling gnawed at me. What if I couldn't throw the ball across the plate? What if I didn't look like a major league pitcher? How bad could I be and still get away with this? I'd intended to go out and throw the ball around some in the days leading up to the commercial, to refine my pitching motion, but the time had slipped away from me. And now here we were, an expensive commercial production resting entirely upon my untested right arm.

About an hour later, the cameras had been set up on risers in center field, which would allow them to shoot me pitching to Bill as though it were an actual televised baseball broadcast. I slowly walked out to the pitcher's mound, secretly dreading what I was about to try to do. It had been raining gently all morning, but the director told us it wouldn't matter; the rain was so light it wouldn't show up on film. Nobody had thought to cover the mound, however, and as I climbed the hill, I realized the tightly packed dirt had devolved into a sticky mud.

I stepped onto the pitcher's mound and gently placed my right foot parallel to the rubber, where it sank a few inches into the sludge. The catcher and the umpire took their places around home plate as Bill stepped into the batter's box. I stood there alone on the mound, and as we waited for the cry of "Action!" my stomach churned. I had assured everyone involved here that I could pitch, that they could count on me to get this job done. I knew nobody would mistake me for Nolan Ryan or Randy Johnson, but I hoped I could at least do Greg Maddux proud and get a pitch up there that Bill could hit into the air.

The rain picked up just as the assistant director yelled "Action!" Because there was a man on base, I came set in the stretch, glanced quickly over my left shoulder at the runner, then rocked and fired the ball home as hard as I could. As I released the ball, my right foot remained stuck in the pool of mud on the mound, and I twisted around and fell hard onto my right side. I glanced up to see my pitch sail over the heads of everyone at the plate and crash about twelve feet high into the backstop fence. My initial thought: Hey, I've got some velocity!

The director called "Cut!" and came sprinting in from center field. I assumed my fall would justify the bad pitch, and it did; the director instead asked me why I didn't throw the ball with a windup. I explained that with a runner on first, a pitcher would never use a windup; instead he'd pitch from the stretch, hoping to hold the runner close to first.

"Well, use a big windup," the director said. "You know, swing your arms around. It'll look better on camera."

I didn't want to argue sports realism in a commercial for a gas station, so I brushed most of the mud off my face, everyone reset, and I went into a heavily embellished windup worthy of Luis Tiant. I may have even swung my right arm around a few times like a windmill. This time I kept my footing, reared back and threw, and the pitch bounced eight feet in front of the plate. The reality, I knew, was that if I did throw a perfect strike, a pitch with speed and control that looked realistic on camera, it would be total luck. And then Bill would have to hit that perfect pitch into the air hard enough that as the ball sailed off screen it would at least look like it had a chance of being a home run. I was operating within the thinnest of margins for error.

After a few more horribly misguided pitches, I decided to stop trying to throw hard and just throw a pitch Bill could hit. I went through the crazy windup, but then at the time of release slowed down a little and just concentrated on tossing a strike. This was my more natural throwing motion, and while I did indeed throw a strike, I threw the ball in a lazy parabola, and it looped slowly toward home plate, resembling nothing like a major league pitcher would throw, instead looking more like a pitch Goofy would throw to Mickey.

To his eternal credit, the director fired me with dignity and calm. After my seventh or eighth completely unrealistic pitch, the director walked up to mound and, one hand rubbing the back of his neck, said, "Okay . . . I think we should give someone else a shot." I agreed and didn't put up a fight, the vision of a handful of hundred-dollar bills dancing in my head. The only problem was that we didn't have any extra players sitting around. Don volunteered that he'd been a pitcher in high school—*now* he told us—so he ended up relieving me, and I went over to become the first baseman. Don immediately went into a windup and zipped a fastball over the plate. Bill swung and hit what normally would have been a pop-up to the outfield, which would suffice as a home run for our purposes. We did some additional shots of Don on the mound with me holding on the runner at first in the background. Before long, all they had left to film was the center fielder leaping in vain for the ball, with the rain continually getting worse, and they dismissed us. I felt rotten. I just wanted to get my cash and get out.

It wasn't until I was almost home that a continuity problem occurred to me. I realized that if Don was going to be the pitcher, he couldn't also be the first baseman in the first shot of the commercial, because in the second shot featuring the pitcher on the mound, the first baseman was visible in the background. But it was too late; we were all gone, cash in hand.

A few weeks later, I was sitting in my apartment working on a story when I heard the Speedway jingle on TV, and I looked up to see our commercial. It began with a shot of first base, where Don was holding the runner on, and then cut to a shot of Don on the pitcher's mound. It was obviously Don in both shots, so I guess they wanted us to think this baseball team employed an identical twin combo. I was barely visible in the background of one shot as a suddenly very white first base-man. (Don, by the way, was black.) The pitch came in, and Bill popped the ball up into the air, and then, incredibly, it landed in a Speedway convenience store, where a group of customers paid the speeding baseball no mind as they shopped for things like hot dogs and beef jerky.

The folks at Speedway must've been happy with what we did, because for the next six months that commercial aired over and over and over. And from then on, every time I heard that catchy jingle—"The convenience stores of . . . *Speed-way!*"—I was reminded of what a failure my baseball career turned out to be.

On the morning of Tuesday, May 9, 1995, the papers in Atlanta were plastered with truly shocking news. Two nights earlier, Bobby Cox had been arrested and charged with simple battery against his wife, Pam. According to the police report, while Bobby and his wife were entertaining guests that Sunday evening, Bobby spilled a drink on the carpet, and an argument followed. The police said his wife tried to push him out of the house, a struggle ensued, and Bobby grabbed his wife's hair and struck her on the left cheek.

Bobby spent the night in jail, and on Monday afternoon the Braves had a press conference at which Bobby and his wife appeared together. "There was no hitting of any sort," Bobby said. "I grabbed her forehead and her hair a little bit just to keep her a distance away from me, and we were both going at it pretty good." When Pam was asked if Bobby had hit her, she said, "No, no."

The charge was eventually dropped, but at least for a few months, it was the preeminent topic in Atlanta. Now, over a decade later, it's not really an issue, at least in Atlanta. "We have one argument in twenty-five years of marriage, and it gets in the paper," Pam Cox told the *Atlanta Journal-Constitution*'s Mark Bradley in 2009. "I'm not proud of it, but we've worked hard to put our marriage back together. I tell the children, 'It's not a mistake if you make it a learning experience.'"

Talking about this failure from Bobby's personal life, the only personal failure we fans ever heard about, still feels weird to me. It happened, sure, but everyone in Atlanta, Bobby included, seemed to move on pretty quickly. Despite it being front-page news, it was none of our business. As much as we'd like to think otherwise, we are often defined by our failures.

Yet this incident would not define Bobby. More than anything, at least in Atlanta, the failure Bobby Cox is associated with is the losing in the postseason. Even though Bobby Cox has won more games than hundreds of baseball managers who came before him, he is still remembered by many as the guy who lost a lot of big games. He made it to the biggest spotlight baseball had to offer, and his Braves stumbled more often than they shined.

The moment I was pulled from the commercial and replaced

with a better fake pitcher was an example of what you could call epic failure. I'd promised everyone they could trust me, that I could handle the job needed to be done. And I fell on my face, literally. I failed in front of my employers and my friends, all caught on tape. Still, mine was a passing moment, embarrassing, memorialized on film, but relegated to some cutting-room floor somewhere; a few minutes that were forgotten soon after, by everyone but me.

As great as the Braves have been, and as often as Bobby is recognized as one of the winningest managers in baseball history, he's also one of the losingest managers of all time—which is mostly just a function of his time served.

Atlanta's consistent losing in the postseason means Braves fans had to confront unprecedented amounts of failure. Not just any old failure, but failure at the highest levels: playoff games, World Series games. And it all happened on Bobby's watch.

There are some people who would have packed up and retired years ago, but Bobby stayed and kept trying to win, kept trying to write a new ending to his story. You fall down, you get up, you try anew.

INTERMISSION

A Comprehensive List of Every Player Who Has Played for the Braves Since 1990, When Bobby Cox Began His Second (Current) Term as Manager of the Braves. The Players Are Ranked Entirely Subjectively, Based on How Much I Liked or Did Not Like the Player.

1. Chipper Jones—For a long time, probably an inauthentically long time, I did not like Chipper Jones. I was a Braves fan when he arrived in '93, and yet I resented him because he seemed to be embraced completely by Braves fans from the moment he was summoned to the majors. I preferred Andruw Jones, in part because Andruw wasn't as fully formed as Chipper was; Chipper could do it all from the moment he arrived, while Andruw, as dynamic as he was, even as a nineteen-year-old rookie in 1996, always seemed to have the potential to become even better. In retrospect, to me, Andruw's potential was more seductive than Chipper's confirmed ability. It wasn't until Andruw left as a free agent after the 2008 season that I was able to enjoy Chipper for all that he was, instead of liking

Andruw for everything he was not. For more on Chipper, see chapter 4.

2. Greg Maddux—See chapter 1.

3. Andruw Jones—See chapter 8.

4. John Smoltz—I flirted with putting Smoltzy at the top of this list. He played twenty years for the Braves, he was our most clutch postseason player, he played through injuries, and he'd undergone more surgeries than any Braves player I could recall. He was also willing to take on different roles in order to help the team, converting from one of the game's most dominant starters to one of its most dominant closers from 2001 through 2004. He won a Cy Young Award in 1996 and was named reliever of the year in 2002. Smoltz eventually retired with 213 wins and 154 saves, the only pitcher in history with at least 200 wins and 150 saves. Smoltz really was the ultimate gamer, sometimes even to a fault, and I always respected him for that. In the winter of 2008, Smoltz left the Braves to sign with the Red Sox, who offered him more guaranteed money than the Braves, and he left as the last member of the 1991 Braves to play in Atlanta. Smoltz pitched part of the 2009 season for Boston and part for the St. Louis Cardinals, then hung it up. Based on his persona while on the field, I always assumed Smoltz would be rather humorless, but during the 2010 Braves season, Smoltz made occasional appearances in the Braves broadcast booth and always told at least one joke per game, which spawned the Facebook page "The corny jokes John Smoltz tells during Braves games."

5. Terry Pendleton—John Schuerholz imported TP from the Cardinals before the 1991 season, and Pendleton was the catalyst for our historic worst-to-first campaign, earning him the league MVP award. His hitting ability was incongruous with his stature: he was maybe five nine, and built more like a refrigerator than a baseball player. I also liked Pendleton because regardless of the weather—if it was one hundred degrees or fifty degrees—TP always rocked what appeared to be a long-sleeved blue sweatshirt under his jersey. You try wearing a sweatshirt for ten minutes in the Atlanta heat and humidity, much less playing an entire baseball season in one.

6. Dale Murphy—My first favorite Brave. Murph was also the first Mormon person I'd ever heard about, and Murphy being Mormon introduced the religion to me and probably throughout Georgia. According to a website called thebaseballpage.com, Dale Murphy's hobbies were:

> Gardening, chess, sailing, ham radio, reading, golf, eating . . . Favorite food: broiled salmon . . . Favorite book: *Baseball's a Funny Game* . . . Favorite TV show: *The Dick Van Dyke Show* . . . Favorite movie: *It's a Wonderful Life* . . . Favorite actor: Jimmy Stewart . . . Favorite music: easy listening and instrumental jazz.

Does it get any edgier than that? Even though Murphy played most of his career as an outfielder, he actually started with the Braves as a catcher. While Murphy had a powerful arm, he had little aim, and when runners would try to steal second, Murphy would sometimes drill the pitcher by mistake. It was Bobby

Cox who moved Murphy to first base and then, later, to the outfield. Many years later, after Cox left for Toronto and then came back to Atlanta as the GM, it was also Cox who traded Murphy to Philadelphia, which nearly caused a riot in Atlanta because Murphy was so popular.

7. David Justice—See chapter 5.

8. Sid Bream—Scored the most important run in modern Braves history. Other than that one run, I don't have many strong memories of Sid, other than of his amazing mustache. It occurs to me as I compile this list: What if Bobby Cox had pinch run for Bream and he hadn't scored that run? How many spots on this list would that have cost Bream? At least thirty, right? Without going back and looking at the box score, the Braves must have been out of bench players in that game, or else there's no way Cox would've left the tortoiselike Bream in the game, knowing he'd have to score from second base on a single. Smoltz, Glavine, Maddux—any of those guys was a faster runner than Bream and probably could have pinch run.

9. Deion Sanders—I understand this might be considered an outrage by many Braves fans, but that's why this is my list and not yours. Deion was one of my favorite football players when he broke in as a corner with the Falcons. He demanded that people call him Prime Time, told everyone that he was going to be one of the most revolutionary athletes of his time, and then went out and actually proved himself. I can understand if Deion's chutzpah turned you off, but to me, a wide-eyed kid, Deion's swagger was like a tractor beam, sucking me in.

In the midst of becoming an NFL Hall of Fame player, he decided he was going to play baseball as well, and somehow the Braves got him. In the end, Deion's egotism probably ended up overshadowing his baseball skills, but he had a remarkably productive Braves career; for his two full seasons, in 1992 and 1993, he batted .290 and had 20 triples. Michael Jordan batted .202 the year he played minor league baseball. Just saying. For more, see chapter 6.

10. Fred McGriff—On the night he arrived from the Padres, two weeks before the trade deadline of the '93 season, all the local TV stations had live remotes down at Atlanta Fulton-County Stadium to cover McGriff's arrival on the 6:00 news. About an hour before the game was to begin, the press box caught fire. As all the media members (and their camera crews) were down on the field talking to McGriff, the entire thing was broadcast live on every local station. This wasn't a small fire in a garbage can, this thing was a raging inferno, with theatrical orange flames leaping toward the upper deck and plumes of black smoke reaching into the sky. There's a video of this event on YouTube (search "Fred McGriff Fire"), and it's just as amazing now as it was at the time. At one point, while former channel 5 sports anchor Jeff Hullinger is describing the scene, a huge explosion comes from the press box. McGriff can briefly be seen laughing and running toward the outfield. The Braves played the game that night, McGriff completed the script by hitting a home run, and the Braves won. Atlanta went on to finish the year 51–19 with McGriff. Yep, I'd say McGriff sparked the team to victory. He really lit a fire under the Braves. With McGriff on the team, the Braves

were definitely combustible. Fred McGriff got the Braves red hot. Enough? Okay.

11. Tom Glavine—See chapter 9.

12. Jason Heyward—See chapter 10.

13. Julio Franco—The Braves signed him for the 2001 home stretch when he was in his midforties, and his arrival in Atlanta (direct from a stint with the Mexico City Tigers) was heralded by an avalanche of stories about the unbelievable shape Julio was in for his age. Former Cardinals and Pirates outfielder Andy Van Slyke openly questioned whether Franco was on steroids, which prompted one of the greatest quotes in Braves history: "Andy Van Slyke is right," Franco told reporters. "I'm on the best juice there is. I'm juiced up every day, and the name of my juice is Jesus. I'm on His power, His wisdom, His understanding . . . Next time you talk to [Van Slyke], tell him the steroid I'm on is Jesus of Nazareth."

14. Brian McCann—McCann came up as part of the Baby Braves movement in 2005, and he quickly supplanted Johnny Estrada as our everyday catcher. Pudgy and constantly dirty, McCann was supposed to be the savvy counterpunch to Jeff Francoeur's power blow. Yet five years after their arrival, Francoeur is gone, and McCann is signed to a long-term deal and was the 2010 All-Star Game MVP. Once Chipper retires, the Braves will probably become McCann's team.

15. Javier Lopez—Lopez was the Braves' best full-time part-time player. I explain all this in chapter 2.

16. Lonnie Smith—One of my favorite Braves nicknames of all time: Lonnie "Skates" Smith, so named because Smith often appeared so uncoordinated when running in the outfield that the only possible excuse could have been that he was wearing roller skates on the field. His nickname was prophetic, as it was a Smith base-running blunder in the '91 World Series that cost the Braves a run and, some would argue, the entire series.

17. Mark Wohlers—We knew Wohlers could throw the ball hard; his pitches regularly reached one hundred miles per hour. That was cool. What wasn't cool was that he couldn't always throw strikes. Okay, he could for his first few years, including back when he was on the '95 World Series champs. But in '98, Wohlers suddenly seemed to forget how to pitch. I was at a game in the late nineties when Wohlers was brought in from the bullpen, and his first warm-up pitch soared over home plate and slammed into the backstop about fifteen feet high. The Braves traded him to Cincinnati a year later, and the day after the trade, the Reds diagnosed him with an anxiety disorder. He eventually returned and pitched relatively well, but he never recaptured what he had in Atlanta.

18. Rafael Furcal—There's something to be said for the allure of youth; that is, at least if I'm doing the talking. For so many years, the Braves had trotted out a bunch of perfectly good baseball players, none of whom was all that explosive. They did their jobs, did them well, and went home. But Furcal was a firecracker, zooming around the bases and displaying probably the best arm in baseball at the time. As a rookie in 2000, Furcal, only nineteen years old, won the Rookie of the Year Award.

I got on the bandwagon early. Furcal was going to carry the Braves in the 2000s. I wanted to be an early adopter. A few years later, we found out that Furcal was actually two years older than he'd been telling everyone. When he became a free agent after the 2005 season, the Braves basically let him go to the Dodgers. It was academic at that point. We almost re-signed him before the 2009 season, but his agent apparently just used the Braves to get a better offer from the Dodgers.

19. Tim Hudson—Considering that Huddy has been one of the Braves' best players for about five years now, I've been curiously devoid of any emotional attachment to him. He ranks this highly not so much because I like him—although I do approve of him—but because I trust him. It's hard to trust baseball players to make the correct decisions the majority of the time. I trust Huddy.

20. Ron Gant—One of the more unusual Braves. He came up to the majors in 1987 as a second baseman and was then switched to the outfield. With his move to the outfield, Gant somehow put on a sizable amount of muscle and turned into a pocket Hercules. Gant found success as an outfielder, and even made the 1992 All-Star Game. Then, after signing a huge contract to stay in Atlanta long term, he broke his femur while riding an ATV in the country outside Atlanta—if nothing else, providing an object lesson to Braves fans about the inherent dangers of piloting all-terrain vehicles. He returned from the busted leg but was not the same and was traded away soon after.

21. Andres Galarraga—El Gran Gato.

22. Gary Sheffield—I was irrationally excited when the Braves traded for Sheff in 2002, because I saw him as something of a spiritual heir to Deion Sanders: an exceptionally talented athlete who wouldn't be afraid to speak his mind. Unfortunately, he was sort of boring as a Brave, toeing the company line. When Sheff's time in Atlanta was finished, and he signed as a free agent with the New York Yankees, Cox said, "Gary, for two years, was pleasant. He's a manager's player. He was terrific. He came to play. Joe Torre will like him a lot." After three years as a Yankee, Sheffield forced a trade.

23. Steve Avery—Part of the Braves' original group of dominant starting pitchers, Avery was the youngest cog and probably the most promising. He also filled the role of the young hayseed not quite ready for the relative glare of the spotlight in Atlanta. Deion Sanders made a big deal of taking Avery under his wing, even going so far as to take Avery shopping to remedy his wardrobe. I loved Deion, but personal shopper just sounds like a bad idea.

24. Marvin Freeman—I have a vague but impenetrable memory of a game in the early nineties when a Braves player was hit by a pitch. Pendleton expected the Braves to retaliate, and when Freeman refused to nail a batter from the opposing team, Pendleton stalked off the field in the middle of the inning.

25. Tommy Hanson—This rangy redheaded righty arrived in Atlanta just a couple of months into the 2009 season. We all knew he was coming, it was just a question of when. Hanson was the one Braves prospect they'd steadfastly refused to discuss

trading, so Braves fans had kept a sharp eye on his progress in the minors, watching him match innings pitched with strikeout totals game after game. As Braves fans, we learned long ago that quality pitching equals wins, and Hanson is shaping up to be the next great piece in our arms race.

26. Otis Nixon—While he had the visage of a cigar store Indian, Nixon was probably the fastest Brave of the Bobby Cox era. When the 1991 Braves were finishing their amazing worst-to-first run, Nixon tested positive for cocaine and was suspended for the World Series. He returned in 1992 and took away a home run from Pittsburgh outfielder Andy Van Slyke in a play now known as "the Catch." I was watching the game and happened to get up to use the restroom, and, as it was the days before Tivo, I missed "the Catch" live. Nixon now runs a ministry outside Atlanta. On the homepage of his website, otisnixon.com, visitors are given two choices: "Enter Site" or "View 'The Catch.'"

27. Steve Bedrosian—Bedrock came up as a starter with the Braves and then was traded to Philadelphia in 1985. The Phillies converted him to a closer. Bedrosian won the Cy Young Award in 1987. He returned to Atlanta in '93 for three seasons to finish his career. I liked him because he always wore his pants cuffed high, exposing his stirrups.

28. Antonio Alfonseca—The Octopus! This was Alfonseca's nickname because he allegedly had an extra finger on each hand. This never got as much coverage as you might assume it would.

29. Martin Prado—Prado spent most of 2010 rising up this list like a bullet. Between 2006 and 2008, Prado mostly shuffled up and down between triple-A and the majors, stuck behind Kelly Johnson in the pecking order at second base, unable to find a permanent slot in the lineup. He finally broke through in early 2009 when Johnson was injured and staked a claim at second. Prado just kept grinding, creating quality at bats and making the best of every plate appearance, batting .307 for the year. (Defensively he played second base, and if you've read this far, you know how I feel about second base.) Yet by the middle of 2010, Prado was starting at second base in the All-Star Game.

30. Matt Diaz

31. Mark Whiten—Perhaps my favorite nickname in modern Braves history: "Hard Hittin'" Mark Whiten. Had an arm that makes Jeff Francoeur look like Jeff Bagwell of the Houston Astros—*after* the perennial all-star's shoulder exploded—but Whiten also seemed to exude a certain laissez-faire that prevented him from winning the hearts of Braves fans. And, apparently, the hearts of Cox and Schuerholz, too.

32. Quilvio Veras

33. Rafael Soriano—One of my favorite Braves' blogs, "Rowland's Office," nicknamed Soriano "BMF." You can look it up.

34. Jair Jurrjens

35. Andres Thomas—I went to one Braves game as a kid and managed to sneak down behind the dugouts because there was nobody at the games then (pre-'91). Andres Thomas shattered a bat during the game, and as he ran back to the dugout between innings, he made eye contact with me and slid the barrel of the bat to me. Weirdly, it was an Omar Moreno–autographed model.

36. Rafael Belliard

37. Gregg Olson

38. Marquis Grissom

39. Kent Mercker

40. Kelly Johnson—See chapter 3.

41. Jeff Francoeur—See chapter 7.

42. Yunel Escobar—Escobar debuted in 2007 and pretty much immediately became a regular in the lineup, playing second, third, and shortstop before settling in as the full-time shortstop in 2008. He was solidly built, athletic, scrappy, with the best infield arm we'd had since Furcal. By 2009, Escobar was occasionally missing signs, making lazy plays, and getting benched. For the first half of the 2010 season, Escobar was hitting a career low .238, and just before the All-Star break, Atlanta traded him to Toronto for journeyman shortstop Alex Gonzalez. For a guy who entered with such promise, batting .326 in his rookie year, it was a rather ignominious exit.

43. Francisco Cabrera—A combination catcher/first baseman who came up through the Toronto Blue Jays organization. The Braves traded for him during the 1989 season, and Cabrera spent

the next few years bouncing between Atlanta and their triple-A affiliate in Richmond, Virginia. In August 1991, Cabrera hit a ninth-inning home run off Cincinnati's Rob Dibble to tie a game that the Braves eventually won in thirteen innings, which kept the Braves in the pennant race and would eventually propel them from worst to first. A year later, during the deciding game seven of the 1992 National League Championship Series, the Braves entered the ninth inning down 2–0. Cabrera had spent most of the year in the minors and had just ten at bats in the majors before this game. Pendleton hit a leadoff double, Justice reached on an error, and then Sid Bream walked. With the bases loaded and no outs, Ron Gant hit a sac fly that scored Pendleton. After another out and a walk, with the bases loaded, two outs, the Braves down 2–1, Bobby Cox inserted Cabrera as a pinch hitter for the pitcher. Cabrera worked the count to 2–0, fouled off strike one, and then laced a single to left field, scoring Justice easily and Sid Bream by the slimmest of margins. Definitely the most famous single in Braves history. Cabrera played one more year with the Braves, then was released in November 1993. He never played in the majors again, but he'll never be forgotten by Braves fans.

44. Mark Lemke—See chapter 3.

45. Rick Mahler—When I was in third or fourth grade, starting pitcher Rick Mahler and his wife visited our church one Sunday morning, apparently looking for a new spiritual home. Our pastor encouraged everyone to welcome them. I welcomed Mahler by asking him for an autograph. At least I waited until the benediction was almost finished.

46. Alejandro Pena

47. Javier Vazquez

48. Charlie Leibrandt

49. Derek Lowe

50. Mike Remlinger

51. Marcus Giles—see chapter 3.

52. Mike Gonzalez

53. Johnny Estrada—When the Braves traded Kevin Millwood in a salary dump during the 2002 off-season, they sent him to Philadelphia for Estrada, a twenty-six-year-old catcher who hadn't even logged 100 games in the majors. While everyone wondered why the Braves couldn't have received more in return, Estrada sat one year backing up Javy Lopez and then replaced him in 2004. Estrada immediately went crazy, batting .314 and making the All-Star team. In June 2005, Estrada was taken out on a questionable collision at home plate by Darin Erstad of the Los Angeles Angels. Estrada suffered a concussion, and while he was out, Brian McCann battled into the lineup. A couple of months later, the Braves traded Estrada to Arizona.

54. Kyle Farnsworth—When the Braves reacquired him at the 2010 trade deadline, my online friend Chuck Norton tweeted that at the very least Farnsworth would improve the Braves chances in the case of a bench-clearing brawl.

55. Robert Fick—While with the Braves in 2003, Fick found an orphaned kitten hiding in a camera well at Shea Stadium while the Braves were in New York. Fick kept the cat and named it Shea.

56. Randall Simon—He was immediately cool because he was the second Braves player from Curacao (after Andruw). Got bonus points for his post-Braves career, particularly his time with the Milwaukee Brewers when he disrupted a sausage race between innings by using a wooden bat to bash the head of a person running in front of the dugout wearing a foam Italian sausage costume.

57. Jung Bong—I always thought this starting pitcher from Korea had the potential to inspire the bestselling jersey (at least relative to the player's statistical success) in Major League Baseball merchandising history.

58. Curtis Pride   60. George Lombard
59. Freddie Freeman

61. Chuck James—Had a brief run as a competent fifth starter for the Braves in 2006 and 2007, but what I liked most was that even while he was in the majors, he held down an off-season job at Home Depot.

62. Mark Teixeira—He was a Brave only for the equivalent of a year, but he had a lasting impact: the Braves had been looking to plug a hole at first base ever since they'd traded Adam LaRoche to Pittsburgh for Mike Gonzalez. The Braves went after Teixeira at the trade deadline in 2007, hoping to make an immediate push for the playoffs. Teixeira was terrific, hitting .317, but the Braves didn't make the playoffs. One year later, at the 2008 trade deadline, with Atlanta out of the race and Teixeira likely to leave in the upcoming off-season as a free agent, the Braves

traded Tex to the Angels for Casey Kotchman. One year later, they traded Kotchman to Boston for . . . Adam LaRoche.

63. Mark DeRosa—Possibly my dad's favorite Brave of all time. DeRosa made the Braves in the early 2000s as a reserve infielder. In 2001, he batted .287 in 184 plate appearances, and then in 2002, DeRosa hit .297 in 232 appearances. Dad couldn't understand why Bobby Cox wouldn't give DeRosa more playing time, and he frequently ended his phone rants about Cox with, "And he's got a .300 hitter sitting on the bench!" I would always point out how, logically, DeRosa wasn't going to unseat Chipper Jones or Rafael Furcal or Marcus Giles, because he wasn't as well rounded a player as any of them. "He's a .300 hitter!" Since then, DeRosa has played for several teams that have given him more playing time. He has not, as yet, finished any season batting .300. (Fine, he hit .296 in 2006.)

64. Oscar Villarreal—One of those guys who came from nowhere, had a solid career as a Brave, then got traded away and completely disappeared. He played two years for the Braves, going a combined 11–3 in 2006 and 2007, and chewing up a lot of innings as a middle reliever. Then Villarreal was traded to Houston and didn't last a full season before disappearing back into baseball's minor leagues.

65. Jorge Sosa   66. Dewayne Wise

67. Jaret Wright—He was a phenom with the Cleveland Indians in the late nineties, before he blew out his right shoulder and couldn't get his fastball back. The Braves traded

for him in 2003, sent him down to the minors, and somehow they reinvented Wright in 2004, when he went 15–8 for the Braves. His contract was up after the season, and he signed with the New York Yankees. Wright's shoulder went out for good a few years later.

68. Mike Stanton

69. B. J. Surhoff

70. Danny Bautista

71. Omar Infante

72. Jarrod Saltalamacchia

73. Brian R. Hunter

74. Ozzie Guillen

75. Rico Brogna

76. Oddibe McDowell

77. Kenny Lofton

78. Casey Kotchman

79. Kerry Ligtenberg—Closer in 1998 and 2000 who cultivated an amazing set of sideburns, making him look either mod or unbelievably stubborn. Ligtenberg was part of the trying collection of closers we had in the nineties. His unconventional last name was a little bit of a problem and, I believe, kept him from being completely embraced by Braves Nation. My dad eventually just started calling him "Lightning Bug."

80. Greg McMichael—Every pitch he threw seemed to be about seventy-eight miles per hour, and seemed to travel on a consistent parabola. You often hear baseball people talk about pitches having movement, but I don't think I've seen anyone who threw every single pitch along the same path, straight in but looping slightly up and then down. Every single pitch.

81. Nate McLouth

82. Ryan Klesko—Klesko, six foot three, 220 pounds, was just a bull of a man. The Braves weren't quite sure what to do with him, constantly shifting him between the outfield and first base. Apparently he now hosts a hunting show on the Outdoor Channel. I always saw him as more of the football fan, the kind of guy who'd take his shirt off and paint his chest at a game.

83. Mike Mordecai   84. Jason Schmidt

85. Ken Caminiti—A former National League MVP (1996), Caminiti came to the Braves halfway through the 2001 season and played just over 60 games. One year later, out of baseball, Caminiti admitted that he'd taken steroids during his MVP season. Simply by looking at his numbers with Atlanta, I feel it's safe to conclude that he did *not* take steroids while a Brave.

86. Dennis Martinez—Had a long MLB career as a top starter with the Orioles, Expos, and Indians, but was mostly known as El Presidente because of his popularity in his home of Nicaragua.

87. Keith Mitchell—The cousin of slugger Kevin Mitchell, Keith was a reserve outfielder on the 1991 Braves. Even though he was only twenty-one years old, he played in the NLCS and World Series. In 1992, flush with outfielders, the Braves sent Mitchell to the minors, and he never played for Atlanta again.

88. Derrek Lee   90. Bill Pecota
89. Jeff Parrett

91. Kevin Millwood—My dad and I just happened to be at his first start in the majors, at a midseason game against the Phillies back in 1997. I'd breezed over something in the paper that morning about Millwood but misremembered his name. On our drive down to Turner Field, I kept talking about this new pitcher, "Millhouse." My dad still calls him Kevin Millhouse to this day.

92. Luis Polonia   93. Eric Hinske

94. Horacio Ramirez—Starting pitcher who briefly showed promise, then was traded in 2006 for Rafael Soriano, which turned out to be a brilliant deal, as Ramirez was released two years later and has bounced around the minors ever since.

95. Charlie Kerfeld   97. Odalis Perez
96. Greg Olson

98. Eddie Perez—Longtime personal catcher for Greg Maddux, and probably the best Maddux catcher we ever had. Perez also had a collection of strange and horrible injuries, from a dislocated tailbone to a ruptured testicle. He's now a Braves coach.

99. Dwight Smith   104. Kevin Gryboski
100. Billy Wagner   105. Clint Sammons
101. Terry Mulholland   106. Pete Smith
102. Michael Tucker   107. Troy Glaus
103. Mike Hampton

108. Buddy Carlyle—Wasn't the most talented starting pitcher, but he ate up a lot of innings in the late '00s for the Braves. Also,

love the story about how at one point the Braves sent him down to triple-A Richmond, and while he was driving to Virginia in a truck with a trailer, the Braves called his cell phone and told him they needed him back in Atlanta. So he executed a U-turn on I-85 and headed back south to The A.

109. Tony Tarasco
110. Jeff Treadway
111. Jonny Venters

112. Juan Berenguer
113. Bret Boone

114. Rudy Seanez—Came from nowhere to be our primary set-up man in the late nineties. This was also around the time that The Rock was rising to prominence in the World Wrestling Federation, and he frequently called people "rudy-poo," to great comedic effect. So Matt and I only referred to Seanez as "Rudy-poo."

115. John Burkett—There was a time when it seemed as though Leo Mazzone could do no wrong as the Braves' pitching coach. Everyone they brought in turned into Cy Young, or so it seemed. Anyway, Burkett had been an all-star starting pitcher in the early nineties with the Giants, then fell on hard times; in the three seasons before signing with the Braves as a free agent just prior to 2000, he'd been a combined 27–33 with a 5.26 ERA. With the Braves, he went 22–18 with a 3.74 ERA, and soon signed a big contract with the Red Sox. Before long his ERA ballooned back over 5.00 and his career ended.

116. Peter Moylan
117. Mike Remlinger

118. Adam LaRoche

119. Edgar Renteria—Toward the end of Renteria's time with the Braves, I realized that I never saw him dive after a ground ball. Maybe this was because the shortstop was just so well positioned defensively that he was always able to get to grounders. Or maybe he didn't like to dive.

120. Brandon Beachy

121. Mike Minor

122. Raul Mondesi

123. Ray King

124. Walt Weiss

125. Charles Thomas

126. Mike Bielecki

127. Pedro Borbon

128. Gerald Williams

129. Cristhian Martinez—This reliever cracks the upper half of my list just for his name alone.

130. Vinny Castilla

131. Paul Byrd

132. Alan Embree

133. Alex Gonzalez

134. Roberto Kelly

135. J. D. Drew

136. Mike Kelly—His most important contribution was that he was called up to the Braves during the 1994 season when the team already had Roberto Kelly, who wore number 12, on the roster. I had been secretly hoping for months that Mike Kelly would make the major league club, because this would give the Braves two Kellys, which I hoped meant they'd have to use first initials on the uniforms. This meant that Roberto Kelly's jersey would read "R. Kelly, 12." And at the time, the singer R. Kelly's unbelievably lascivious album *12 Play* was atop the charts and causing controversy. I just thought that would be funny. But they never added an *R.* to Roberto

Kelly's jersey, and Mike Kelly got sent down after 30 games. Clearly, if blogs had existed back then, I would have been very popular.

137. Wilson Betemit   138. Terrell Wade

139. Willie Harris—I like any baseball player with a gold tooth.

140. Brian Jordan   144. Mike Cather
141. Bobby Bonilla   145. Jody Davis
142. Rick Ankiel   146. Joe Boever
143. Brad Clontz   147. Bruce Chen

148. Denny Neagle—He was a good starting pitcher, winning 20 games for the '97 Braves, known for his uncanny ability to imitate a train whistle. Unfortunately, I have a lot of information like this taking up space in my head.

149. Roberto Hernandez   154. Reggie Sanders
150. Takashi Saito   155. Kenshin Kawakami
151. Joe Borowski   156. Russ Springer
152. Brooks Conrad   157. Jose Cabrera
153. Tony Graffanino   158. Charlie Morton

159. Jose Capellan—Hard thrower in the minors who was supposed to be a top prospect. The Braves ended up trading Capellan for Brewers closer Dan Kolb. Capellan pitched five seasons in relief but never stuck with any team, and he's out of baseball now. I sure did draft him way too high in my fantasy league.

160. Jermaine Dye
161. Russ Ortiz
162. Melky Cabrera
163. Chris Reitsma

164. Will Ohman
165. Eric O'Flaherty
166. Tyler Yates
167. Brayan Pena

168. Ryan Langerhans—We share part of a name; I had to pull for him.

169. Mark Kotsay
170. Jorge Campillo
171. Kris Medlen
172. Jo-Jo Reyes
173. Wally Joyner
174. Will Cunnane
175. Kyle Davies
176. Steve Karsay
177. Garret Anderson
178. Ron Mahay

179. Darren Bragg
180. Jason Marquis
181. Damon Hollins
182. Tyler Houston
183. Brent Lillibridge
184. David Ross
185. Damian Moss
186. Geronimo Berroa
187. Damon Berryhill

188. Jay Powell—He was thirty-seven years old and on his sixth major league franchise by the time he arrived in Atlanta in 2005. During a game toward the middle of the season, Powell threw a pitch and horrifically broke his arm from the force. I was watching the game when it happened. One of those moments you don't forget. Ever.

189. Tim Spooneybarger
190. Danny Heep
191. John Thomson
192. Jose Ortegano

193. Jay Howell
194. Mike Bell
195. Sean Bergman
196. Tony Castillo

197. Dwayne Henry

198. Tommy Gregg

199. Chris Brock

200. Ed Giovanola

201. Jordan Schafer—I'm not sure where he'll be playing when this book is published, but he's already had a wild career. Drafted by the Braves in 2005, Schafer was tremendous in the minor leagues. He led all of the minors in hits in 2007, and Braves fans had high hopes for him in 2008. Then he was suspended for 50 games for, according to ESPN.com, "use of human growth hormone in violation of the minor league drug prevention and treatment program." Schafer quickly claimed his innocence, telling the *Atlanta Journal-Constitution* he'd been suspended for "being caught hanging around a bad group of people." Whatever, he returned and had a strong second half in 2008, and then made the Braves major league team coming out of training camp in 2009. In his first at bat, on opening night in Philadelphia, Schafer drilled a long home run to center field. Yet soon it was obvious he wasn't ready for the majors—he was striking out a little more than one-third of the time. Fifty games into his major league career, he was sent back to the minors, where a wrist injury eventually required surgery. Who knows how he'll turn out? He's still only twenty-four years old.

202. Andy Ashby

203. Jim Clancy

204. Norm Charlton

205. Steve Lyons

206. Trey Hodges

207. Melvin Nieves

208. Joe Hesketh

209. Micah Bowie

210. Pablo Martinez—We obviously had the wrong P. Martinez.

211. Derek Lilliquist

212. Milt Hill

213. Brent Clevlen

214. Greg Myers

215. Jorge Fabregas

216. Tommy Greene

217. Chad Fox

218. Dean Hartgraves

219. John Hudek

220. Diory Hernandez

221. Juan Cruz

222. Dave Gallagher

223. Doug Sisk

224. Kevin Lomon

225. Darrell May

226. Jesse Chavez

227. David Nied—At one point, he was supposed to be our top prospect, until MLB introduced the Rockies and the Marlins in 1993. In the expansion draft, Colorado made Nied the first overall pick, the cornerstone of its new franchise. He pitched two full seasons, parts of two more, then never played in the majors again. Guess the Braves knew what they were doing when they left him exposed for the draft.

228. Michael Dunn

229. Octavio Dotel

230. Tim Spehr

231. Mark Grant

232. Sergio Valdez

233. Josh Anderson

234. Tony Peña—He is actually the son of longtime Pirates catcher Tony Peña, who used to catch basically sitting on the ground with his right leg kicked way out to the side. I was at a Braves-Pirates game as a kid in the eighties, and following a game, probably a Braves loss, I went down behind the Pirates dugout to try to get a baseball or some sort of paraphernalia from a player or a ballboy or whatever. Peña Sr. looked over the dugout, made eye contact with me, gestured for me to wait a second, disappeared into the dugout, and came back out a few

moments later and slid one of his signature-model bats across the roof of the dugout to me. It had a slight crack in it, nothing visible, but it was something I've always cherished. (By the way, the bats from Peña and Andres Thomas are the only two bats I got at games. Don't worry, no more bat stories.) In 2007 the younger Tony Peña (a shortstop, incidentally) moved on to Kansas City, the team his father managed for three-plus seasons from 2002 to 2005. In 2009 he was converted to a pitcher.

235. Rey Sanchez
236. Steve Torrealba
237. Macay McBride
238. Henry Blanco
239. Ernie Whitt
240. Ruben Gotay
241. Boone Logan
242. Rico Rossy
243. Wilfredo Ledezma
244. Dan Meyer
245. Albie Lopez
246. Eli Marrero
247. Bernard Gilkey
248. Craig Kimbrel
249. Steve Colyer
250. Dave Martinez
251. Scott Proctor
252. Daryle Ward
253. Matt Whiteside
254. Matt Murray
255. Manny Acosta
256. Trey Moore
257. Mike Devereaux
258. Will Startup
259. Phil Stockman
260. Kevin McGlinchy
261. Sam McConnell
262. Barbaro Canizares
263. Danys Baez
264. Kurt Abbott
265. Brandon Jones
266. Ken Ray
267. Royce Ring
268. Kevin Barry
269. Tanyon Sturtze
270. Shane Reynolds
271. James Parr
272. Nick Green
273. Brad Woodall
274. Jeff Ridgway
275. Steve Reed
276. Joe Winkelsas

277. Andy Pratt
278. Matt Franco
279. Chris Seelbach
280. Wes Obermueller
281. Chris Resop
282. Joe Slusarski
283. Lance Cormier
284. Anthony Lerew
285. C. J. Nitkowski
286. Scott Kamienieki
287. Stan Belinda
288. Don Wengart
289. Luis Rivera
290. Jim Brower
291. Mike Sharperson
292. Jose Ascanio
293. Andy Marte
294. Gregor Blanco
295. Greg Colbrunn
296. Mark Davis
297. Adam Bernero
298. Jerry Willard
299. Jerome Walton
300. Ryan Church
301. Kelly Mann
302. Vladimir Nunez
303. J. C. Boscan
304. Todd Hollandsworth

305. Freddy Garcia—There were two Freddy Garcias: one who pitched for a decade in the majors, was an all-star, and once led the AL in ERA and innings pitched. And then there was *this* Freddy Garcia, who had three at bats with the Braves in 1999.

306. Marc Valdes
307. Chris Hammond
308. Marty Clary
309. Darren Holmes
310. Jairo Asencio (Luis Valdez)
311. Fernando Luna
312. Blaine Boyer
313. Armando Almanza
314. Seth Greisinger
315. Roman Colon
316. Elmer Dessens
317. Todd Pratt
318. Reid Gorecki
319. Matt Childers
320. Armando Reynoso
321. Jose Oliva
322. Joe Ayrault

323. Wes Helms

324. Matt DeSalvo

325. Jorge Julio

326. Brandon Hicks

327. John Foster

328. Tim Drew

329. Marty Malloy

330. Jorge Vasquez

331. John LeRoy—I don't remember LeRoy, but his page on Baseball-Reference.com is sponsored by someone named Mario Lanza, who left this message: "Best pitcher I ever played against. I was 0-for-my-lifetime against him, and I played left field behind him during a no-hit, 15 k game he threw in '92. No one could touch him. He got a win in his only ML appearance. RIP, John, you will be missed."

332. Randy St. Claire

333. Paul Marak

334. Justin Speier

335. Ismael Villegas

336. Everett Stull

337. Rusty Richards

338. Pascual Matos

339. Travis Smith

340. Victor Rosario

341. Jarvis Brown

342. Brian Barton—In 2008 Barton, an outfielder, played in 82 games with the St. Louis Cardinals. After the '08 season, the Braves traded reliever Blaine Boyer for Barton. In 2009, Barton played 1 game in the majors with the Braves. He entered as a pinch runner and was immediately caught stealing. He stayed in the game in right field for the final two innings, caught the one fly ball that was hit to him, and hasn't played in the majors again.

343. Steve Sisco

344. Tom Martin

345. Aaron Small

346. Frank Brooks

347. Adam Butler
348. Cory Aldridge
349. Jason Perry
350. Ramon Caraballo
351. Joe Nelson
352. Pedro Swann
353. Tom Thobe
354. Derrin Ebert
355. Rick Luecken
356. Jimmy Kremers
357. Gabe Molina
358. Mike Heath
359. Mike Hubbard
360. Tim Unroe
361. Dave Stevens
362. Francisley Bueno
363. Alexis Infante
364. Trent Hubbard
365. Rod Nichols
366. David Cortes
367. Wayne Franklin

368. Jesse Garcia
369. John Ennis
370. Terry Clark
371. Jason Shiell
372. Ben Rivera
373. Ray Holbert
374. Brian Edmondson
375. Brian Kowitz
376. Joe Dawley
377. Carl Schutz
378. Howard Battle
379. Scott Sobkowiak
380. Dan Petry
381. Julian Tavarez
382. Greg Norton
383. Jim Presley
384. Jim Vatcher
385. Charlie O'Brien
386. Mike Hessman
387. Chad Paronto

388. Jeff Bennett—He had a few good seasons as a righty reliever, but he always seemed to give up hits in the clutch, giving my dad and me numerous cases of indigestion. The Braves sent Bennett down to their triple-A team in 2009. When my dad went to see his first Braves triple-A game, who was the first reliever brought in to pitch? Jeff Bennett.

389. Willy Aybar

390. Keith Lockhart

391. Joey Devine—The Baby Braves roared into the 2005 National League Division Series against the Houston Astros, so it was only fitting that in game four, with the series on the line, the ball ended up in the hand of twenty-one-year-old rookie reliever Joey Devine. In both of his first two appearances in the majors just months before, he'd allowed grand slams, becoming the first player in major league history to allow such damage. Still, Bobby being Bobby, Cox included Devine on the postseason roster. He made a perfect two-batter appearance in the Braves' game one loss, then gave up two hits, a walk, and a run in the game three loss. When game four stretched into the eighteenth inning, with the Braves' bullpen emptied out, Cox brought in Devine, who fell behind 2–0 to Houston's Chris Burke. On the next pitch, Burke homered, giving Houston the win and knocking Atlanta out of the playoffs. They hadn't been back to the postseason until 2010. Before the 2008 season, the Braves traded Devine to Oakland.

392. Jeff Reardon

393. John Rocker—You may have heard that John Rocker made some controversial comments a few years ago. That's probably enough said.

394. Paul Bako—Played a little over a full season with the Braves as Maddux's personal catcher and batted .205 over that time.

395. Craig Wilson	397. Scott Thorman
396. Mark Redman	398. Bob Wickman

399. Nick Esasky—Before the 1990 season, the Braves signed first baseman Esasky as a free agent from the Boston Red Sox after a season in which Esasky had hit 30 home runs with 108 RBIs. The Braves gave him a contract that, at the time, was considered huge (three years, $5.6 million). Esasky started the first nine games of the season, hit .171 with no home runs or RBIs, and then announced he was suffering from vertigo brought on by an ear infection. He never played pro baseball again. So that signing didn't work out so well.

400. Pete Orr   401. Jose Hernandez

402. Dan Kolb—Acquired by the Braves in the 2004 off-season to be our closer, since Smoltz was going from the bullpen back to the starting rotation. Kolb finished the 2005 season with a 3–8 record and 11 saves in 57 innings pitched. Less than a year after trading for him, the Braves somehow convinced Milwaukee to take Kolb back.

403. Chris Woodward—He was a reserve infielder for the Braves throughout the 2007 season, and somehow he stayed on the roster the entire season, even though he batted .199 with 1 home run. Bobby kept getting him at bats, waiting for him to turn it around. He couldn't.

404. Corky Miller—In 2008, he batted .083. The Braves had eight pitchers that season with higher batting averages.

405. Jeff Blauser—Blauser missed the 1995 World Series, the only one we won, with an injury. Had two great career seasons,

1993 (.305 BA) and 1997 (.308 BA). Those two seasons also just happened to come when the shortstop was in the final year of a contract. After that '93 season, Blauser posted three subpar seasons, despite being one of the highest paid players on the Braves. He snapped out of this for the 1997 season, with a new contract on the line. After that second huge year, the Braves said thanks but no thanks and let him walk. Blauser signed with the Cubs, where his batting average dropped almost one hundred points down to .219. A year later he managed to improve it to .240 before retiring.

CHAPTER 6

GREATNESS: How Deion Sanders
Is Like Ted Turner

Selected men from popular culture who played important roles in shaping my adolescent life:

1. Michael Jackson, singer, 1983–87—I was at Lenox Square mall in Atlanta with my mother one day when we walked past a Coconuts record store. Prominently positioned in the front of the store was a pyramid made from copies of Michael Jackson's *Thriller* album. Not having ever watched MTV or listened to pop radio, I knew only that Michael Jackson was very popular at the time, so I went in and bought the record, the first music I'd ever purchased on my own. I went home and played it on my parents' hi-fi stereo system, listened to it for a few weeks, then went back to that same store and bought a copy of the same album on cassette tape so I could listen to it outside when I was shooting hoops or throwing a baseball against the wall of the house. I must have listened to *Thriller* at least five hun-

dred times. When *Bad* came out in 1987, I bought the tape at the Richway department store on North Druid Hills Road, but I wasn't as into that album.

2. Run-DMC, hip-hop group, 1987–89—My friend Shuford introduced me to rap music through Run-DMC. I later branched out into LL Cool J, DJ Jazzy Jeff & the Fresh Prince, Public Enemy, Dana Dane, Kool Moe Dee, and others. In 1988 my friend Todd and I saved our money and attended a touring rap show when it played at the Omni arena in downtown Atlanta. The headlining act was Run-DMC, and the opening groups included Public Enemy, EPMD, DJ Jazzy Jeff & the Fresh Prince, J. J. Fad, and others. More than any other type of music, hip-hop informed my musical tastes, and for me it all stemmed from Run-DMC.

3. Davey Boy Smith and the Dynamite Kid (aka the British Bulldogs), WWF tag team champions, 1988–90—In middle school I became obsessed with professional wrestling. Every Friday night, channel 36 in Atlanta aired an eight-hour block of wrestling shows it called *Superstars of Wrestling,* and I watched as much as I could stay awake for. Hulkmania and the initial eighties wrestling explosion had ended, and now pro wrestling was more about feuds and factions than entertaining the audience, especially the younger audience. This was particularly true of *Superstars of Wrestling:* most of the programs were obscure regional promotions from around the South, with basically no production value. The British Bulldogs were in the WWF, so they were nationally known. They were tough, athletic, and innovative, and I admired their grit and tenacity. I also

really liked Ricky "The Dragon" Steamboat, until "Macho Man" Randy Savage hit him in the throat with the ring bell and put him out of action for an extended time.

4. Dominique Wilkins, small forward, Atlanta Hawks, 1989–93—After a lifetime of admiring basketball from afar, I began playing and watching the game constantly. Dominique might not have been the best player in the NBA, but he was the best player on the Hawks and we always believed he was close to being on the level of Michael Jordan or Magic Johnson. He never reached that level, but Nique was still our "Human Highlight Film."

5. Deion Sanders, center fielder, football cornerback, and television analyst, 1991–present—Deion had been a standout college football player at Florida State University who was drafted by the Atlanta Falcons. He was not only a dominant football player, but he liked to remind us about his brilliance, constantly, to the point where it was mildly annoying even to me, one of his biggest fans; I can only imagine how excruciating it must have been to those who didn't like him. Deion began dabbling in baseball during the NFL off-season, and after a stint in the New York Yankees organization he was acquired by the Braves in 1991, one of the greatest days of my life: my favorite football player could now be my favorite baseball player, too.

On the football field, within that context of anger and machismo, Deion's bravado was minimally more acceptable. But on a baseball diamond, he was like a firecracker in tight pants, pretty much exactly the opposite in demeanor and disposition from the Braves' most popular players—Terry Pendleton, Tom Glavine, and John Smoltz—who were so businesslike in their approach they could've played in suits. Bobby Cox was in charge, this fatherly figure who wouldn't know Deion's buddy MC Hammer if he were sitting in his lap. Meanwhile, here came Deion, an earring dangling from his earlobe, drawing dollar signs in the dirt when he came to bat.

So it fell to me to root for Deion, and I had no problem with this; for some reason his persona just clicked with me. I had all his signature Nike shoes, his T-shirts, several posters, and, even after he left the Braves, I obtained a copy of his 1994 rap album *Prime Time,* featuring the singles "Prime Time Keeps Tickin'" and "Must Be the Money." The more Deion alienated Braves fans and the local media, some of whom seemed to intensely dislike having to cover his antics, the more I embraced him. He was obviously a promising baseball player, and to me that was the most important part. That liking Deion made me seem countercultural was a bonus.

Just a few years ago, I was assigned to write a magazine profile on Deion, and I spent a day following him around the New York studios of CBS Sports, where he was working as an analyst on *The NFL Today.* When we were just sitting and talking, he was funny, insightful, and even asked me questions about writing and my life covering the NBA. But when the red light went on, he almost physically morphed into "Prime Time," this gregarious, boastful character who couldn't be too outlandish if he tried, and try he did. To me the delineation was as obvious that day as it was in the early nineties, but to most of Atlanta back then, Deion was a riddle. One of the first things I asked Deion was about the way he was perceived back then.

ME: Nobody seemed to be able to figure you out, especially the papers and local TV stations. Why didn't the media understand you?

DEION: Because I was a complex black man. Being the first in years to come out and do it the way I did it. And not only that—my game backed up my name. A lot of people who came out like I did didn't have the guts to back it up. But my game backed it up. So they [the media] said, "Shoot, what can we say about this guy? We gotta attack his character. Because we can't attack his game. We can't sit him down and put a microphone in front of his face and not have him articulate his way out of it." So I could verbally whup 'em and I could physically whup 'em. So they had to attack my character.

ME: But you kept giving them ammunition, dressing like you did, talking smack like you did.

DEION: Oh yeah, yeah. But they didn't say anything about the other dudes when they came in cowboy boots and Wrangler jeans, when they came in their get-up. But when I came in my get-up, it was on.

A few days later, I got a voice mail at my office from Deion. I'd given him my card, not really expecting to hear from him, but he'd called and left me his number and said to give him a call if I needed anything else for the story or had any other questions. A day or two later, I had a few follow-up questions prepared, so I gave him a call, and Deion issued an open invitation for me to visit him on another Sunday broadcast. A few weeks after that, my wife and I were out doing some Christmas shopping in midtown Manhattan one Sunday morning, and I persuaded her to swing by the CBS studios. We spent less than an hour with Deion, but in that time we saw him take delivery of a floor-length mink coat, tape a segment in which he presented Christmas gifts to a group of angelic children while in character as "Sanders Claus," and playfully accost former NFL coach Jerry Glanville, demanding that Glanville turn over a sack full of biscuits from a Popeyes fast-food restaurant.

I have met Ted Turner twice in my life. The first time was in the winter of 1998. Turner still owned the Hawks and the Braves at the time, and had recently announced the addition of the Atlanta Thrashers, a National Hockey League expansion team. Turner's empire, Turner Broadcasting System, had recently merged with AOL. At the time, nobody was really sure what this meant; it just seemed inconceivable that a billionaire's cable news and sports companies were of a value on par with a buggy email client best known for sticking free CD-ROMs in every paper and magazine. Because Ted remained a fixture at games and events around town, it seemed at least initially as though things were going to remain the same.

At the time, my personal future was about as murky as that of the Atlanta teams. The first year I wrote full-time for a living was 1997, and I totaled about $12,000 in income. I'd managed to jam one foot in the door at *Creative Loafing*, Atlanta's longtime weekly free alternative newspaper, which was then the second-largest newspaper in Georgia behind the *Atlanta Journal-Constitution* in terms of circulation. Because the first person I'd made contact with at *CL* was the music editor, and because the urban music writer happened to have just left the paper, I was quickly appointed its urban music columnist and spent two years writing weekly features and interviews about music, mostly R&B and hip-hop.

I stumbled into a serendipitous situation. Atlanta was just on the verge of becoming the urban music capital of the world. But throughout this time, despite the constant activity on my beat, what I really wanted to do was write about sports. I could never feel about music the way I felt about sports. I loved music, and played guitar and sang in several bands years earlier, but I'd watched sports every day of my life for twenty years. I would never know what it felt like to freestyle sixteen bars, but I could write from experience about the pressure of facing a 3–2 pitch with the bases loaded. Particularly about how it feels to strike out in that situation.

To break into the sports section of *Creative Loafing*, I initially looked for ways to combine music and sports. When New Orleans–raised rapper and entrepreneur Master P was playing preseason basketball with the NBA's Charlotte Hornets, I went to a Hawks game to interview him. I entered the locker room a few hours before the game, and P was the only player there, already dressed in his complete uniform and sitting plaintively in front of his locker. He invited me to pull up a seat, and we sat and talked for a while. I got a great look at his teeth, which were each sleeved in gold, with an ornate series of diamonds and rubies inset. One Hawks staffer told me, "His teeth are worth more than I'll make in my entire life." After much badgering, the Hawks eventually gave me a seasonlong press credential, and soon after they asked me to write for the monthly in-house magazine they produced for fans and sponsors. I freelanced profiles of the different players, and it was harder than you might think to come up with ways to make marginal role players sound heroic.

In the winter of 1998, the Hawks and Thrashers broke ground on what was to be their new home, Philips Arena. The Hawks asked me to cover the ceremony for their magazine, and it was basically just a quick press conference featuring short speeches from Turner employees and executives from Philips, the Dutch electronics giant working its way into the United States. But Ted Turner himself was also there: fast-talking, larger than life, and glad-handing everyone in attendance. They'd set up Philips flat-screen televisions all over the event; at the time, these were extremely rare.

After the press conference, I noticed Turner standing alone, staring intently at a monitor, as though by staring at the television he could see its inner workings. I approached him, introduced myself, and said I was working on an article for the Hawks' magazine about the partnership announcement. He never made eye contact with me, so mesmerizing was this flat-screen television, but Turner ad-libbed a perfect press release quote: "Aw, I'm glad to be associated with Philips, because everything they do is great stuff."

I thanked him and before walking away paused to check out the television myself. I'd never seen a flat-screen television in person, and I circled it slowly to see it from all angles.

"A flat TV!" Turner marveled to me. "Man, this is red hot! That sucker is flat!"

As an athlete and as a persona, Deion Sanders was as dynamic as it got. As an Atlanta Brave, he just never quite fit. While the Braves could tolerate a certain amount of flash and panache, Deion didn't seem to have an off switch. I still recall the moment he made me a believer: during a televised spring training game, Deion was on second base when someone hit a long fly ball into the right-field gap. The center fielder drifted over and caught the ball, and Deion tagged up and took off toward third base. Knowing that he didn't have a chance at throwing out Deion at third, the outfielder lazily lobbed the ball back toward the infield. Deion raced for third, never slowed, and turned for home, picking up speed. As the ball reached the cutoff man, Deion sprinted across home plate. Deion had tagged from second and scored easily on a routine fly ball. And that was just in spring training.

Deion was constantly pulling off these crazy athletic feats, things improbable and fantastic but probably ill advised. As a Deion acolyte, I knew the history by heart before I interviewed him. I asked him if it was true that he'd run a blistering 4.19 forty-yard dash while wearing his full football pads. "Naw," Prime Time said. "What happened was I ran a 4.25 in spikes. And then they said, 'You have to take off the spikes.' So I took off the spikes, put on tennis shoes, and then ran a 4.21. Then I looked at them and said, 'Now take that!' "

After Deion dumped ice water on CBS analyst Tim McCarver during the 1992 NLCS celebration, his days as a Brave were numbered. McCarver had been hypercritical of Deion's commitment to the Braves during the NLCS. McCarver was so shocked by Deion's liquid retribution that all he could muster was a few shouts of, "You're a real man, Deion! A real man!" That incident highlighted Deion's gift and his curse. When you got Deion, you got the total package.

In John Schuerholz's book about how to become a successful leader, *Built to Win: Inside Stories and Leadership Strat-*

egies from Baseball's Winningest GM, Bobby Cox is asked about Deion, and he describes him thusly: "Deion was for one thing—himself. He was into promoting himself as that football-baseball combination—the first guy to ever do this or that. It was all about Deion. And he didn't want to participate in our duties off the field: going to luncheons, fan photo days, things like that; responsibilities that come with being a Braves team member."

Coming from Bobby Cox, this kind of criticism is about as harsh as it gets, but it doesn't discount Deion's talent. In 1992 Deion played in 97 games for the Braves and batted .304. In the 1993 World Series, he played with a broken bone in his foot and still batted .533. And can we also acknowledge that it's likely no Braves players have ever enjoyed going to luncheons or fan photo days? Maybe Deion was just worse at hiding his dislike than everyone else. If you watched tape of him hosting *Saturday Night Live* in 1995, as I have, multiple times, you would know that for all of Deion's gifts, acting isn't foremost among them.

In early 1994, the Braves traded Deion to Cincinnati for Roberto Kelly. Even without Deion, the Braves kept right on rolling, although they did finish only second in that strike-shortened season. As Schuerholz summed up Deion's Atlanta career in his book: "Good player. Good riddance."

The players we identify with identify us as humans. Being a fan of a player is like joining a political party; wearing his jersey is the equivalent of planting a sign in your front yard. Supporting a player isn't just hoping he does well, it's admitting that you share some fundamental common ground with said athlete. Deion Sanders may not have been the most accurate reflection of the values I held important, but he was the greatest athlete I'd ever seen, and I was willing to overlook his personal flaws so that I could tell the world I was aligned with someone so capable of athletic transcendence.

Say what you want about Deion—many have and many will, including Deion. You don't have to approve of his style, of the way he supposedly valued self over team. But when he arrived in Atlanta from Florida State University, he did make maybe the most important contribution to the Braves fan culture in modern Braves history, however unwittingly.

Because without Deion, there's no tomahawk chop.

Back in 1984, the crowd at a Florida State University football game began singing a song called "Massacre" that the marching band frequently played. They eventually incorporated a chopping motion with their arms—similar to a referee signaling for a first down. Deion played at FSU, and when he joined the Braves in 1991, some Braves fans began doing the chopping motion and singing the droning tune for Deion. It quickly caught on, and even after Deion left to join the Falcons, this hymn remained. For us fans, as the '91 Braves went from worst to first, it was our rallying cry, something you could do even at home as those Braves continued to defy logic and fears, night after night.

And for whatever reason, it stuck. Now known as the Tomahawk Chop, even today, two decades later, the moment the Braves begin putting together a rally, out comes the Chop. If you're a fan of another franchise, I'm sure the Chop can be annoying. But it is what it is. It's now as much a part of the Braves as Bobby Cox or Chipper Jones. And as a fan of the Braves, even twenty years after it was introduced, it's still pretty awesome to be in a full Turner Field when 45,000 fans all start doing the Chop in unison.

One day in 1999, the editor in chief of *Creative Loafing* gave me a call and asked me to lunch; I had no idea what this was about and immediately wondered if I'd done something wrong. I'd just started to get to know Ken Edelstein, who was a tremendous journalist, a writer who massaged every word before it went to print. He'd slowly been incorporating me more and more into the paper, having me write an occasional sports column and edit a page about participatory sports in and around Atlanta. Whenever I'd come by the office, I'd relay to Ken whatever local gossip I'd overheard. Eventually I wrote a few cover stories for *CL*, about everything from college football to a local community-owned radio station, and I spent a lot of time with Ken parked in front of the computer fine-tuning those, going over every noun and verb, making sure it all belonged. I'd always had a knack for telling a story, but Ken was teaching me to really love the process of writing. For a few years there, Ken was my Bobby Cox.

I met Ken for lunch at some vegetarian restaurant befitting a liberal alternative newspaper's editor in chief. Every issue of *Creative Loafing* opened with a news-and-gossip column called "Talk of the Town." It was the first thing you saw when you opened the paper; the most prominent real estate. For years, the column had been written by Tom Houck, an Atlanta legend who'd been involved in city politics and media for decades. Ken told me that Tom was leaving, and Ken wanted me to give the column a shot. I couldn't say yes quickly enough. Ken was interested in the circle of Atlanta that I represented. I was in my midtwenties and suddenly I was the lead columnist for the second-largest newspaper in Georgia.

The first few months, I was flying blind, but I kept going out, showing up at events, shaking hands, making phone calls, and before long, I was given entrée to a larger slice of Atlanta than I ever knew existed: I ate at great restaurants, was invited to concerts, met Atlanta's leading politicians. For a twentysomething kid, it was heady stuff. People passed along tips to me, and I chased down stories, week after week.

Ted Turner remained Atlanta's biggest name. When I took over the column, Turner and Jane Fonda had recently split, though nobody seemed to know exactly why or what was going on. In the spring of 2000, CNN celebrated its twentieth anniversary by throwing a huge party in Centennial Park in downtown Atlanta, just outside the CNN Center. I attended the party to cover it for the paper, and I attended it with my future mother-in-law, Sara, who at the time was the president of the Georgia Hispanic Chamber of Commerce. Ted's publicist introduced us. When Ted learned Sara was Hispanic, he asked the woman with him—who we later learned was his girlfriend at the time—to "throw some Spanish at her."

I asked Ted if he spoke any Spanish.

"No, no," he said. "You don't have to be smart to make a lot of money, you know. I would learn Spanish, but . . . well, number one, I can't hear very well. And number two, I'm not very smart. So that's two strikes against me right there."

My mother-in-law was well regarded politically in Atlanta, and she served on a board with Jane Fonda, whom she'd gotten to know pretty well. She mentioned to Ted that Jane was a great lady.

"Yeah, she is," he said, then paused. "I've been divorced twice, you know, and it's always my fault. No matter what happens, it's always my fault. Have you ever been divorced?"

Sara replied that she had been, once.

"So, you know what it's like. Probably wasn't your fault, though."

I told Ted that I'd never been married and asked what advice he'd give me.

The richest man in town gave me a sly smile and said, "Don't do it. Don't." He started to walk away, then spun back around. "No, do get married. Do it. That's what I'd tell you. I'll get married again, if I can find the right person."

A few days later, I flew up to New York to interview for a full-time job at *SLAM* magazine. A few months prior, Sara's daughter Isabel had accepted a full-time job in Manhattan at Time Inc. We'd been dating for over a year and were desperately in love. She wanted me to come with her.

I was completely torn. I'd been doing the column in *Creative Loafing* for about a year, and it was picking up momentum. I'd been freelancing regularly for *SLAM* from Atlanta, which gave me the chance to flex my sportswriter muscles from time to time. When Isabel got the official job offer to move to New York, she called and told me she was going to take the gig. I hung up the phone and placed a call to New York to Russ Bengtson, the editor in chief of *SLAM*. Russ and I had become friendly over the course of my time writing for *SLAM*. I mentioned my conundrum, and Russ said that *SLAM* had an opening for an online-editor job that I could have if I wanted it. I hung up, called Isabel back, and told her I'd gotten a job in New York, too.

I still wasn't sure I wanted to leave Atlanta. Life had suddenly become easier. For the first time in years, I knew I was going to be able to pay my rent each month; knew I wouldn't be late on a car payment. At the same time, I felt a tremendous sense of loyalty to Ken and *Creative Loafing.* They'd plucked me from obscurity and placed me on a platform to give me a voice in Atlanta. So I worked hard to find something interesting to say each week. And Ken had patiently nurtured me, teaching me everything I could learn about journalism and the newspaper business.

When I finally told Ken about the decision I was struggling to make, he said he really wanted me to stay and wanted to talk more about it, but in the end, for me, what it came down to was this: I had been given a lot in Atlanta, but I hadn't really asked for any of it. Things were just starting to happen. By no means did I live an opulent life—I didn't have insurance, for instance—but life in Atlanta was suddenly no longer such a fight. And I wasn't eating ramen and Mountain Dew for dinner six nights a week.

There were two things I really, really loved during my life in Atlanta: sports and Isabel. And now I was being told that if I wanted to keep Isabel in my life, I'd have to move to New York City. And while I was there in the greatest city in the world, I would be paid to watch and write about sports?

Yes, please.

One thing the Braves under Bobby Cox have become known for is churning out capable coaches. From Ned Yost to Jimy Williams to Fredi Gonzalez, Bobby's lieutenants have consistently left the nest and spread their wings elsewhere.

And we haven't even talked about Leo Mazzone, the man who shepherded the incredible Braves pitching staffs. During Mazzone's fifteen years as pitching coach, the Braves' pitching staff was first or second in the National League in team ERA a dozen times, won six Cy Young Awards, and posted nine 20-game winners. ESPN.com selected Mazzone the best assistant coach of all time in any sport. He eventually left Atlanta in 2005 for Baltimore, where his longtime friend Sam Perlozzo was the manager.

As I got more experienced and started working with other writers, I was always surprised to hear from writers who got upset when anyone changed a word of their copy. Look, I always tell writers, none of us is Mark Twain here. If I'm editing your copy, it's not for the fun of it. I'm trying to make you better. If anyone else has a suggestion, I'm all ears. I trace this personal literary glasnost back to my time at *Creative Loafing,* the hours I spent sitting with Ken in his tiny office shoehorned around his computer, going word by word through my stories to find the best, most evocative language to get facts and feelings across.

In my experience, the best leaders are people who aren't afraid to take input and listen to others. Ted Turner will be remembered as one of the greatest businessmen in American history, but I'm willing to venture he didn't reach such mind-boggling success without help along the way from his trusted lieutenants. When Turner first bought the Braves, he was a hands-on owner, even managing one game in 1977. But it wasn't until he let Bobby Cox take over that the Braves became the Braves dynasty we know.

From the sound of things, as an Atlanta Brave, Deion wasn't considered a leader. And yet I think Deion learned from his time with the Braves, only it wasn't readily apparent until you look at his football career: After leaving the Atlanta Falcons in 1993, he signed a one-year contract with the already-stacked San Francisco 49ers. The team promptly won Super Bowl XXIX, and its new cornerback was named NFL Defensive Player of the Year. A year later, Deion took less money than other teams offered to sign with the Dallas Cowboys dynasty, where over the next five seasons he won another Super Bowl. He could have gone to less talented teams and made more money, but he saw the value in winning and got the championships he didn't get with the Braves.

I don't know exactly how Bobby Cox has managed his staff, but it doesn't seem likely that so many people with transferable talent would have come and worked for Bobby unless they felt valued. The other managers who have spent as much time in baseball, Bobby's contemporaries like Tony LaRussa and Joe Torre, are known for their own accomplishments, not as much for other coaches they nurtured who went on to different franchises. As talented and legendary as he is, Bobby obviously hasn't had a problem working with great people, listening to them, or sharing credit with them, which is something all of us could probably stand to remember.

CHAPTER 7

ADAPTING: How Jeff Francoeur
Is Like Teaching Yourself to Cook

In this era of almost lawless free agency, athletes who play their entire professional careers in just one city are increasingly rare. And athletes who play their entire careers in their hometown are even more uncommon. Cal Ripken Jr., for instance, played and lived in the Baltimore area his entire life. Joe Mauer was born and raised in St. Paul, Minnesota, and he currently stars behind the plate for the Twins. Playing your entire career in your hometown requires both luck and talent: for starters, you have to get drafted by your hometown team and you have to be good enough that your team doesn't ever want you to play for anyone else. For fans, seeing a guy grow up in your backyard and not only actually make it to the big leagues but also become an everyday player and then an all-star is the rarest of sports experiences, right up there with winning a championship.

In the summer of 2005, the Braves summoned two hometown guys from the minor leagues: a pudgy catcher named Brian McCann and a sweet-swinging, cannon-armed outfielder

named Jeff Francoeur. Both had grown up in the Atlanta suburbs and played on local Little League teams. In the 2002 amateur draft, the Braves took Francoeur in the first round and
McCann in the second. They progressed through the Braves'
minor league system simultaneously, then were summoned
from the minors to Atlanta within one month of each other.
Francoeur's first game with the Braves was a doubleheader
against the Chicago Cubs. In game two he started in right field,
and in the bottom of the eighth inning, the twenty-one-year-
old rookie blasted a three-run homer to seal a 9–4 Braves win.

Immediately, it felt like something electric was happening.
While Bobby Cox always thrust rookies into the lineup almost
as soon as they set foot in the majors, presumably in order to get
them playing before any nerves had a chance to develop, "Frenchy" appeared to be more than a stopgap. The Braves desperately needed help in the outfield; Francoeur was in right field
to stay. Francoeur's high school career as a baseball and football
star at Parkview High School had been well chronicled in the
Atlanta Journal-Constitution through the years, and his perfor-
mance in a state championship football game had been televised locally. By the time he reached the major leagues, Atlanta
sports fans knew of Francoeur's name, exotic as it was.

What we weren't sure about was his game. After high school,
Francoeur disappeared into the Braves' farm system for a few
years before emerging that July night at Turner Field, direct
from the Braves' double-A squad in Jackson, Mississippi. His
debut was an undeniable star turn, but could someone really
come from a mid-level minor league team and arrive in the
big leagues as a fully formed major league star? Was Francoeur
really our long-term answer in right field following the losses

in consecutive years of the powerful yet temporal right fielders Gary Sheffield and J. D. Drew? We wanted to believe in Francoeur, especially after what we'd been through.

It's important to remember that Sheffield and Drew had each been acquired via trades and had arrived in Atlanta as proven, if fickle, all-star-level talents. Drew, who also grew up in Georgia, had originally been drafted by the Phillies but refused to sign for the amount of money they were offering; instead he played semipro ball for a year, reentered the draft in 1998, and ended going in the first round to the St. Louis Cardinals. Since then, he'd been injury plagued, never playing more than 135 games in a 162-game season. Sheffield was a converted infielder who had been an all-star several times before coming to Atlanta, but he was regarded as a malcontent, having played for four franchises before the Braves. Both players, however, remained healthy, behaved, and played some of their best baseball for Bobby Cox. And then took off.

In 2005 the Braves began the season with Raul Mondesi in right field as a hobbling reclamation project. This was at best a wild hope against hope, and it wasn't surprising when Mondesi could not return to the form that saw him win Rookie of the Year a decade earlier; the Braves let him go just a little over a month into the season.

And then came Francoeur, who sprang up out of nowhere like a dandelion. With his perpetual five o'clock shadow, stirrups yanked high, his eye black permanently smudged, Francoeur immediately looked the part of an old-school baseball player, like he'd just stepped out of a Bowman baseball card from the 1950s. His play also pegged him as a throwback, continually hustling, always swinging for the fences, a reminder to many fans (like my dad, who immediately adopted Francoeur as his favorite player) of a time when baseball wasn't populated by what they perceived as loafing millionaires but by energetic kids and average joes who held down nine-to-fives in the off-season. Francoeur played so effortlessly, and his skills seemed to have developed so organically, that some fans started calling him "The Natural."

Most important, Francoeur seemed like he was loving the whole ride. He was constantly smiling and laughing and cutting up. Francoeur and McCann lived together in a bachelor pad, where it was wholesomely reported that they sat around playing video games all the time. A few months after the 2005 Braves season ended, I went to the heated University of Georgia–Georgia Tech football game at Georgia Tech's stadium in midtown Atlanta. I knew Francoeur had been a star football player in high school, so I wasn't surprised when my friends pointed out a bearded Jeff Francoeur there at the game. What *was* surprising was that Francoeur was sitting just a few seats down from us, toward the top of the lower level of seats, mixed in with everyone else. The beard disguised him a little, but not such that we didn't notice him pretty much immediately. Still, people seemed to be leaving him alone and admiring him from afar, as if we were proud of our local kid who had, to borrow a Southern colloquialism, done good.

When I decided I wanted to write a book about the lessons I'd learned from Bobby Cox, a friend suggested that I read a book called *Julie & Julia,* which details a blogger's life as she tries to cook every recipe in Julia Child's *Mastering the*

Art of French Cooking. I bought the book, read about thirty pages, but never picked it up again. Little did I know I'd end up writing a chapter about food and cooking. After all, it was only minutes after Isabel and I moved in together that I discovered she could not cook. I don't mean that she was simply a below-average chef, or that she was incapable of seasoning food properly, or that she was unable to precisely measure baking ingredients. No, she really knew absolutely nothing about cooking. Put her in a kitchen, she could burn water, undercook cereal, blacken air.

The truth is, I was just as bad. My cooking expertise included dishes like grilled cheese sandwiches, omelets, and nothing else. At least I was doing my part to keep the dairy industry afloat. I don't know if at some previous moment in my life I'd fallen back on outmoded gender delineations and simply assumed that the woman I'd marry one day would feed me, but to me food was strictly fuel—something to get me through the day. Which meant I'd power lunch at McDonald's or Wendy's, then maybe have a Hot Pocket or ramen noodles for dinner. Mountain Dew was my main source of liquid nourishment, at least until I discovered how delicious Starbucks's Frappucinos could be. When I felt an urge to be healthy, I'd go out and get a salad smothered with plenty of crunchy artificial bacon bits and croutons and creamy dressing. Fast food fast became my best friend.

Isabel has strong memories tied to food. When you grow up with your mother and grandmother, both Cubans, living in the same house, food abounds. Isabel still talks about her grandmother's *picadillo*, a traditional Cuban salty-sweet dish, almost like an olive- and raisin-studded beef and tomato stew. Whenever we visit Miami, where her grandparents settled after leaving Cuba, all we do is eat at Cuban restaurants, so Isabel can, if even briefly, relive those taste memories, flavors, and smells.

I have those memories as well, although perhaps not as intensely. I remember my grandmother making fried chicken using found ingredients—corn flakes, for instance—as a crust, and my grandfather eating creamed chipped beef on toast for breakfast. My mother would fix flank steak, the most affordable cut, every Sunday after church. My dad refused to eat onions, and my mom wasn't a big fan of garlic, so we ate a variety of dinners prepared completely without aromatics. My mom, even to this day, when she has nothing better to do, will cook or bake. She worked full-time while I was growing up, yet she cooked dinner every weeknight, and baked cakes and cookies on the weekend. She was an excellent chef, but she seemed to enjoy baking more.

While I did not develop an appreciation for the subtleties of food, I did observe the dedication required to put it on the table every night. My mother had a bookshelf overflowing with cookbooks, everything from church congregation–made recipe compendiums to books about the basics of regional cuisine published by *Southern Living*. All told, there must have been thousands of recipes available, and given the amount of butter and sugar called for in most Southern recipes, a combined 27.6 million calories in those books. Recently I called my mom and asked if she had any ideas for Southern recipes that could be scaled down into hors d'oeuvres for a dinner party Isabel and I were hosting here in New York. Within twenty minutes, my mom emailed me four recipes that she suspected could work in such a setting, including a potato salad calling for an entire package of bacon, and a chicken salad recipe that suggested incorporating two cups of crushed potato chips.

Recipes like these recall the church potluck dinners I attended growing up, when they'd ask people to bring varied dishes so they wouldn't end up with all the same foods—and then everybody would bring fried chicken and deviled eggs anyway. (Both parts of the chicken were being fully exploited.) Nobody would bring a light salad, a starch, a fruit plate. Instead we'd have folding table after folding table covered with fried chicken and deviled eggs. Eventually, if memory serves me well, a sign-up system was adopted in order to avoid future potluck menu fiascos. It was understood that this took the luck out of Southern potluck, but it was a sacrifice we all had to make.

For the first month that Isabel and I lived in New York, we had dinner delivered every night. One evening, on the way home from work I stopped at a grocery store a block from our apartment. This market was a far cry from the palatial Kroger and Publix supermarkets I'd grown up with. In Atlanta, even the smallest grocery stores were huge, sparkling warehouses stocked with any food you could imagine. In New York, because of spatial constraints, most grocery stores are about the size of convenience stores back in Georgia. At this store the items were stacked floor to ceiling, usually in some illogical, haphazard order. And if you found something you liked, there was no guarantee you would ever see it there again. Going to your local grocery store in Manhattan with a specific shopping list in hand is like playing the lottery. Looking for an "exotic" food item like, say, cilantro? Pearled couscous? Curry powder? Cross your fingers and pray. The upside to this is that the things in the store are usually fresh. I once bought a bunch of rosemary, got home, and found a worm still living on one stem.

As I carefully squeezed my way through the cramped aisles, stepping over the stacks of cans waiting for a home on the shelves, being careful not to turn too quickly in any direction for fear of my backpack knocking over a shelf, I wasn't sure what I was looking for. My arsenal of recipes was completely empty; actually, it had never really been stocked. A dusty cardboard box high on a shelf caught my eye. It read, Arroz con Pollo. Hey, I'd had this one! Chicken with rice, a traditional Cuban dish! And here were all the ingredients I would need to make this in one convenient box—including, I swear, a can of chicken—with instructions on the back? Done!

That evening I learned that no matter how closely I followed the suggested recipe, food from a box does not taste anything like what anyone's mom and grandmother used to make. Unless the family lived in a bomb shelter.

In his first 30 games in the major leagues, Jeff Francoeur batted .373 with 10 homers, 28 RBIs, and a 1.144 OPS. Yet for everything there was to like about Francoeur, he wasn't perfect. Mostly, his pitch selection wasn't very, uh, selective; it is in no way an exaggeration to say that he seemed to swing at every pitch thrown to him. (He finished his rookie year with only 11 walks in 274 at bats. And three of those were intentional.) It was almost as if Francoeur had never faced any pitchers who intentionally threw him a pitch he couldn't reach. So rather than be patient, work the count, wait for his pitch, he just swung as though he were being paid by the swing. Other than his inability to differentiate between balls and strikes, Francoeur had it all: power, speed, defense.

At first, Francoeur's quirks just made him more intriguing. While he was an athletic six foot two, 225 pounds, he used a bat that looked to be too big for him. He swung this bat as though it were ablaze and only a vigorous stroke could extinguish the fire. The ferocity of his swings combined with the size of the bat gave him the appearance of swinging a club, which led Chipper Jones to bestow upon him the temporary nickname "Captain Caveman." Cox's less expressive but more predictable at-bat tag "Frenchy" eventually won out.

If nothing else, Francoeur was gutsy. In 2004, while playing for the Braves' single-A affiliate in Myrtle Beach, South Carolina, Francoeur squared to bunt a pitch. As he turned and faced the pitcher, the ninety-five-mile-per-hour fastball hit him near his right eye, causing multiple facial fractures and seriously endangering his baseball future. Francoeur recovered in time to be called up to the major leagues the next season. Then, in the off-season after his rookie year, Francoeur blew his nose so hard that he dislodged a piece of cartilage and caused an infection that required him to spend nearly a month taking antibiotics through an intravenous drip.

After he took Atlanta by storm, the rest of baseball took notice. Francoeur was such a sensation that *Sports Illustrated* put him on the cover of its August 29, 2005, issue with a cover line that screamed: "The Natural: Atlanta Rookie Jeff Francoeur Is Off to an Impossibly Hot Start. Can Anyone Be This Good?" The actual story inside focused more on the Baby Braves, which was just as satisfying. As the Braves had won thirteen consecutive division titles, they'd relied on the same group of veterans:

Chipper, Smoltz, Andruw, Glavine, and so on. Then, in 2005, everyone began falling apart all at once. Desperate for bodies, the Braves turned to their farm system. Over the course of the season, twelve rookies made their major league debuts and eighteen rookies received playing time, including Francoeur and McCann. Despite—or maybe because of—the influx of youth and inexperience, the Braves finished 90–72 and basically skipped and hopped their way to a fourteenth consecutive division crown. For us Braves fans, it was a singularly fun experience. We'd become accustomed to winning through experience and reliability. Bobby had always been there with his steadying hand, but to win with youth and enthusiasm was unusually invigorating.

As for Jeff Francoeur, the undisputed face of the Baby Braves, *SI* noted that he "seemingly can do anything on a ball field." But one note of caution was sounded by Chipper Jones, who pointed out, "Add fifty, sixty walks a year to what [Francoeur will] put up, and the sky's the limit."

At the time, this felt true. Reason tells us that no player can have an extended major league career without being selective at the plate: pitchers will eventually figure out that the guy will swing at anything close to the strike zone, and they'll simply stop throwing hittable pitches. But at the same time, there was so much about Francoeur that defied traditional baseball logic. Who really knew? Maybe he would be able to have a long, productive career without altering his method. After all, it was that unconventional approach that made him exciting.

We will never know if Chipper was correct. Francoeur never recorded 50 walks in a season; his high was 42 in 2007. To contrast, Chipper has never had fewer than 60 walks in a season.

And to *Sports Illustrated*'s original caps-locked question, "Can Anyone Be This Good?"

As it turned out, no. Or at least Jeff Francoeur couldn't.

He followed up the 2005 explosion with a slow decline. As David O'Brien pointed out in the *Journal-Constitution,* in 310 games following the 2007 All-Star break, Francoeur hit .256 with just 25 homers, 153 RBIs, and a .304 OBP and .381 slugging percentage.

To parse, Francoeur hit 10 home runs in his first 110 at bats, and then 25 home runs in his next 1,195 at bats.

Once it became apparent that Francoeur could not and would not redefine the basic tenets of hitting developed over a hundred-plus years of baseball, we waited with increasing impatience for him to adapt. In 2008, with the Braves' enthusiasm waning, they sent Francoeur back down to Mississippi for a weekend to work with his former coaches. By the 2009 season, the Francoeur situation was taxing everyone. While Bobby publicly professed nothing but confidence in his young charge, the Braves tried to teach Francoeur patience. For him to be an above-average outfielder, it was obvious to everyone except maybe Francoeur that he'd have to make a change. He just couldn't continue to confront every pitch with hellacious swings. Could he?

Finally, a week after the Fourth of July, the Braves basically gave up: They traded Francoeur to the archrival Mets. The kid who had once been the toast of baseball was traded for reserve outfielder Ryan Church, whom the Braves let walk away when the season ended.

In his final months with the Braves, Francoeur talked often about how uncomfortable he was trying to alter his approach to hitting. His reasoning, he said, was that his philosophy—swing often and swing hard—had brought him to where he was, and if anything, he felt he needed to swing even more than before. No matter how he tried, Jeff Francoeur just couldn't change.

During the time that I was discovering the power of food, I ingested two meals that forever illuminated this world for me.

1. In the fall of 1999, not long after Isabel and I started dating, I had the opportunity to accompany her on a press trip to Budapest, Prague, and Vienna. Isabel had been steadily working to broaden my horizons, to refine my rougher edges, and I think she hoped this trip would make me a little more continental. I will admit that I probably didn't help things get off to a good start when, during a lunch in Vienna at an elegant restaurant with several public relations people who were hosting us, I repeatedly leaned back in my chair, and later may or may not have audibly belched after eating my entrée.

    In Prague, some American expats we'd met recommended that we have dinner one night at a place called Palffy Palace. It wasn't listed in any of the dozen or so guidebooks Isabel had brought along, and I could not find any mention of it on the internet, either. All we had was an address on a piece of paper, written in a language that looked completely unrecognizable. Our cab driver seemed as confused as I was by the address, as we drove around aimlessly all over downtown Prague. Just as I began to wonder if the driver remembered that we were actually in the back of the car, he pulled up outside what looked to be an old castle, fronted by two monstrous wooden doors.

Inside, on the second floor, we found Palffy Palace. The castle turned out to be a music school, and each evening one large classroom was converted into a five-star restaurant. The room was lit entirely by candlelight; soft classical music played; the waiters wore dark suits and white gloves. It was like stepping into a dream.

Just looking around the dining room, I immediately became suspicious. How much was this meal going to cost? If there's one thing I've learned from being with Isabel, it's that luxury never comes cheap. And if it does come cheap, one way or another you'll probably get sick afterward. What I forgot was that we were in the Czech Republic, where the economy at the time was even worse than the U.S. economy is now.

I don't recall exactly what we ordered that evening, probably because the first bottle of wine I ordered was one of the most expensive on the wine list and it cost only about $8. As brilliant and lavish as this restaurant was, it was practically giving food away. Several years later, my experience was accurately replicated in the movie *EuroTrip* by several characters who find themselves in Slovakia with just $1.83 to their name, only to find that this immediately made them among the richest people in the country.

It was either fortune or destiny that my sudden ascension into society's highest class coincided with this culinary awakening. We ordered the six-course prix fixe menu, and I'm pretty sure the meal began with caviar and toast. I had tasted caviar before, but this was the first time I'd *appreciated* caviar; cherished the briny, grainy bubbles bursting in my mouth with each bite. The one dish I recall with clarity was my entrée, a baked whole salmon in a champagne-mustard sauce. I ordered this because it sounded as though I'd be comfortable with it: I knew what mustard was, I knew what champagne was, I knew what salmon was. I liked the way all these things tasted by themselves, and it seemed logical that all of these ingredients would taste good in concert with one another.

I flaked off some salmon, dunked it into the moat of sauce, chewed and swallowed, and almost immediately, I *got* it. The candles, the music, the overattentive waiters—that stuff was amazing enough. But the food I ate that evening made everything in my life, for that one evening, just a little bit better. Our conversation was sharper, the air felt a little cooler, people seemed a little friendlier. It was my first encounter with food as a transformational experience.

2. Not long after we moved to New York, the company that runs *SLAM*, Harris Publications, started a men's magazine called *King*. It was a men's magazine, but it was presented with a much more urban bent than anything else on the market. One night while watching the Food Network, I saw a segment on a young chef in Manhattan named Marcus Samuelsson. He had an incredible backstory: born in Ethiopia, orphaned by a tuberculosis epidemic, adopted by a Swedish family. And he'd made himself into one of the best chefs in New York. His restaurant, Aquavit, got a three-star review from the *New York Times,* making Marcus the youngest chef in the paper's history to earn that honor.

A few weeks later, I showed up at Aquavit one morning to interview Marcus for a small piece in *King*. I was wearing a Paris Saint-Germain soccer jersey and my Braves hat, and instead of talking about cooking and food, Marcus and I ended up talking sports for about an hour. We were about the same age, and we hit it off.

After we finally got around to discussing food, Marcus invited Isabel and me to have dinner that evening at Aquavit. I went home and ironed my only suit, using the toilet seat in our tiny apartment as an ironing board, and dug a pair of dress socks out of the bottom of my closet. When we arrived at Aquavit, Marcus came out and greeted us and asked if there was anything we were allergic to, as he had a special menu planned for the two of us. I may not have had any medical allergies to food, but I had some deep-seated emotional allergies to certain ingredients.

For instance, I'd adopted my father's onion odium. I'd spent my entire life avoiding onions, in any shape or form. Considering my diet, this usually meant scraping the onions off cheeseburgers at McDonald's. Avoiding a specific food item, particularly one as prevalent as the onion, required constant vigilance. I understood that disliking a food, any food, wasn't completely sensible. And the onion? The onion is one of the oldest vegetables known to man. Billions of people eat them every day and enjoy the taste. I had nothing against the flavor, nothing against the texture. I just couldn't approve of the *concept* of onions. It was almost as though I was boycotting onions for whatever it was they'd done to my father so many years ago.

After getting to know Marcus and having examined his

accolades, I had no choice but to concede that preparing food was something Marcus did better than almost every other person in the world, that he was gifted at figuring out which foods tasted the best when put together. And that evening, I decided to put my taste buds in Marcus's capable hands. If he served me something that I thought I didn't or wouldn't like, Marcus wasn't doing it to frustrate me, he was doing it because these foods belonged together and he was implicitly suggesting that I, as a reasonable person, should recognize that these flavors were complementary or possibly even transcendent.

We had a transcendent meal. And ever since that night, I've eaten pretty much anything that comes my way.

Except bananas. I still hate bananas. I haven't grown up that much.

B ecoming a foodie required releasing a lifetime of rules I'd painstakingly developed over twenty-five years, or 9,125 consecutive days. If food is life, I wasn't living the best life that was available to me, but I finally realized it. Since I expanded my horizons and embraced all the options available to me, I've found unexpected pleasure and unwanted pounds in food.

Similarly, it was obvious to everyone, probably even eventually to Jeff Francoeur, that by not adapting to some simple precepts even casual baseball fans had picked up on, he wasn't being the best baseball player he could be.

Bobby Cox has never been known for his flexibility; if anything, it's been the opposite. For instance, why does he always pull the starters too soon and the relievers too late? This makes it even more satisfying when he *does* do something unconventional and out of character, like sending up a pitcher to pinch-hit or putting on a shift against a pull hitter. During game five of the 1991 National League Championship Series against the Pirates, twice Cox had Tom Glavine intentionally walk Bobby Bonilla to bring the struggling Barry Bonds to the plate. Cox put the pressure squarely on the then skinny shoulders of Bonds, who'd hit 25 home runs with 116 RBIs during the season but had gone a combined 3 for 15 in the series up until then. Both times that Cox forced Bonds's hand, the Braves got him out. Atlanta ended up losing the game 1–0, then winning the series with Sid Bream's iconic slide.

To me the most enduring legacy of Bobby's adaptability is best and most simply observed by looking at the list of pennants won, contrasted with the list of names in the Intermission of this book. There are no Braves players left from Bobby's first teams (1978 to 1981), and now Chipper Jones is the only player left from the nineties; the second-longest-tenured Braves are Brian McCann and Tim Hudson, who both joined in 2005. Bobby has had literally hundreds of players wear a Braves uniform under his management, but somehow they kept on winning.

There have been some amazing players during that time, as well as some players I shudder to remember. But somehow Bobby has maximized their abilities, using his tried-and-true system of managing. Everyone knows what's coming. Until they don't.

Criticize Bobby for being inflexible all you like, but the truth is, you don't win 2,504 games without being able to adapt when the time is right.

CHAPTER 8

COMMUNICATING: How Andruw Jones
Is Like Your Grandmother Dying

It was the hottest day of the summer—July 9, 2007—and I was at work in Manhattan when I found out that my grandmother had just died. I'd had jury duty that morning, then had checked in at the office for a while. Just as I was heading home, my mom called from Atlanta. Nana Evelyn was dead. She was one hundred years old.

She was my father's mother. I never met my father's father— he passed before I was born—but I grew up around Nana Evelyn. My other grandparents, Paw Paw and Nana Carolyn, lived in Alabama, but Nana Evelyn lived in Atlanta. So I saw Nana Evelyn regularly, to swim at the pool behind her condo or have dinner at one of those buffet-style restaurants that older people frequent. Nana and I didn't have anything in common, really, other than we were related. She didn't like sports or hip-hop or writing, so when we talked, it was mostly about her life, the things she'd seen and experienced. Despite her longevity, she was sick a lot, in and out of hospitals and nursing homes and hospices with vague illnesses. She'd get really sick, to the point where we thought the end was near, and then she'd make these incredible recoveries and be fine for years and years.

A few years before she died, she'd spent months gravely ill in a nursing home. Once again, Nana Evelyn improved to the point that she wanted to move into a retirement home, into her own apartment with her own kitchenette. At the retirement home, she was active—even started "jogging" every day. When I pressed her on jogging, it turned out she was just going outside for walks each day. I guess she thought jogging sounded cooler. Either way, it was impressive, considering that she was about ninety-five years old at the time. She made friends with several of the women there, and she enjoyed having afternoon drinks with one of her neighbors. One day she unexpectedly asked my mother to get her "marijuana mix." After some investigation, we learned what she really wanted was margarita mix.

The last time I saw Nana Evelyn was maybe two months before she died. I was in Atlanta for a weekend, and instead of spending a Sunday with Bobby in person at Turner Field, I went to the nursing home to spend some time with Nana. She was terribly frail, so old that her skin was tearing in places. Her breath smelled stale, and I realized that she was probably unable to brush her teeth. Nana was in a wheelchair when I arrived, completely immobile. With considerable effort, she grunted the words "living room."

I pushed her chair from the bedroom into her little apart-ment's living room, locked the wheels, and just started talking, not so much to her as *at* her. I don't remember what I said, but I just wanted to keep talking to mask the crushing silence in the room. A few minutes later, she again asked me to take her to the living room. Which was where we already were. So I pushed her in a circle around the coffee table and parked her exactly where she'd been before. This seemed to satisfy her.

She didn't react to anything I said all day, until I got up to leave, and she reached out and motioned that she wanted to give me a hug and a kiss. Which she did.

I never saw her alive again.

I must have been five or six years old when sports discovered me. It wasn't like I'd been avoiding them—surely I had heard of baseball, basketball, and football, though I didn't understand any of the rules or tenets of those games. But that was a different era than the one we live in now. Cable TV was new and exciting, and the twentysomething channels my family received on our one television were mind boggling. At the time, *SportsCenter* had just come on the air, and ESPN showed more cheerleading contests and log rolling competitions than anything else. Living in Atlanta meant that the Braves were constantly on Ted Turner's fledgling TBS channel, before it was a self-anointed "Superstation." Still, at that time, when sports were on TV, more than anything, I was just upset that cartoons or *The Great Space Coaster* had been bumped.

Kickball was the first organized sport I recall participating in, off at a summer camp. I didn't know what kickball was, how to play, any of that, so I had one plate appearance, recorded an out, and then sat quietly on a picnic table and watched the rest of the game, not understanding that "out" meant I wasn't actually disqualified from participating in the game. A few weeks later, back home in Atlanta, I realized that despite having logged time in an actual game, I *still* didn't know how to play kickball. One afternoon I broached this topic with my mom and asked her if she could explain kickball to me.

This is the kind of thing most kids would probably ask their father about, but my dad was different. I knew he liked sports, and I'd seen him watching golf, football, and basketball on TV and yelling along, but since I had never shown an interest in sports, he hadn't pushed them on me. He wasn't like some fathers that you hear about, overtly athletic or scarily obsessive about any particular team—we had no bumper stickers on our cars. More than players and teams, my dad was into the numerology of sports. He liked studying numbers, then complaining about the Hawks not shooting enough high-percentage shots or, more recently, about Bobby Cox consistently refusing to play reserve infielder Mark DeRosa.

Numbers were my dad's sport. He pored over box scores and created elaborate fantasy games, drafting teams and playing full schedules long before the internet came along and we all joined rotisserie leagues. While he was in the army during the 1950s, stationed in New Orleans, Dad used his downtime to develop a system—using a deck of playing cards—that would somehow allow him to replicate entire golf tournaments using probabilities based on existing statistics. His crowning achievement remains his golf league, which he will proudly tell you is currently in its forty-first year. All of the professional golfers are divided into squads, and they compete in a yearlong competition that Dad meticulously tracks using playing cards, a calculator, and graph paper. As this was started prior to the internet and *USA Today,* at one point Dad subscribed to a variety of niche golf magazines so that he could get all the scores, even if they were a week or two late, in order for his stats to be complete. He named his golf league NOLA in honor of its birthplace (New Orleans, LA). He's since created NOLA baseball, basketball, and indoor football leagues, among others. And though I now deal with sports statistics every day as part of my job, I am still completely perplexed by his system and how it operates.

Every weekday while I was growing up, my dad went to work. He ran the computer accounting system for a small empire of men's clothing stores called Muse's Clothing, once an Atlanta landmark known as "the Style Center of the South" during the fifties and sixties. Muse's saw its business slowly erode in the nineties as corporate America began strangling the little guys. While I was in college, Muse's filed for bankruptcy protection, and my dad was forced into early retirement.

I don't know if he worked hard at his job, because I never really saw him in action there. I do know, however, that he worked regularly, always gone from nine to six, and when he came home, he would invariably spend time playing with my sister and me. He did not love his job, he has since told me, but he did it every single day to provide for the rest of us. His silent actions then still speak loudly to me today.

The night my grandmother died, I called home to Atlanta to check in on everyone, but I didn't get a chance to speak to my dad. I flew home a few days later and ran the gauntlet of seeing the extended family, attending the graveside service, moving all of Nana's furniture out of her room at the retirement home and into my parents' attic, and then, finally, the memorial service.

I started crying during the ceremony at the cemetery, which I hadn't anticipated happening; for some reason, it was hearing the words "we return her to the earth" that made me tear up.

I needed a break. We all did. My father is generally pretty upbeat, but even he seemed a little quiet, depressed. It had been a week of moving, crying, remembering, planning, wondering. Something had to break the cycle. Thank God the Braves were in town.

Dad and I found our seats at the top of Turner Field's section 201 around six fifteen, a little less than an hour before the first pitch and about four hours after Nana's memorial service had ended. It was "Christmas in July" night at the stadium, which added a completely random wrinkle to the proceedings. It also explained why I'd seen a girl dressed like a reindeer on my way into the park.

I purchased my hot dog and roasted peanuts; Dad got a cheeseburger and a bucket-sized Coke too big to fit in the cup holder mounted on the seat in front of us. This remains the largest drink container I've ever seen; Dad needed two hands to carry it. Out on the field, Bobby Cox wobbled out to present an oversized check to an animal care charity. Dad and I settled in and got to work picking everything apart.

In the bottom of the first inning, Andruw Jones stepped to the plate. For so many years, Andruw was my favorite player on the Braves. This has long been a point of silent contention between my father and me. Bobby Cox always calls Andruw the best center fielder he's ever seen, and I haven't found any evidence to the contrary—by most accounts, nobody in the history of baseball has ever been as good defensively as Andruw was in his prime. But, offensively, there were problems.

Despite his raw talent, Andruw's inconsistency at the plate prevented him from breaking through to superstardom, to the level of an Alex Rodriguez or a Barry Bonds. When he was younger, Braves fans unanimously believed he was going to become unstoppable. At nineteen years old, late in the 1996 season, Andruw was called up to the Braves from Richmond. Andruw began that season playing A-level ball, on one of the Braves' lowest-level farm teams. Playing there he hit 17 homers and had 16 stolen bases in 66 games. He then moved up a level to double-A, where he played in 38 games and had 12 homers and 37 RBIs. The Braves dutifully bounced him up to triple-A—remember, this was all still the same season, when Andruw was only nineteen. In Richmond, Andruw played just 12 games, but he hit 5 homers and knocked in 12 RBIs. The Braves finally brought him up to the majors in time for the postseason, where he hit two home runs in game one of the 1996 World Series against the New York Yankees, making him the youngest player in the history of baseball to go deep in the Fall Classic.

The moment I first saw Andruw in a Braves uniform, I gravitated toward him for reasons I didn't fully understand. I'd never seen him play before, had no idea what he looked like, but I knew he was being heralded as the next Mickey Mantle or Junior Griffey, so he had to be pretty good. I was almost giddily attracted to Andruw. And I will admit, part of it was that I have always just liked the way "Andruw" is spelled. I understand that the spelling of an athlete's name should not have any bearing on my appreciation for him as an athlete, but for some reason it totally does. It's just a cool name. The next dog I get, I'm naming it Andruw.

I was twenty-two years old and, for the first time in my life as a sports fan, I found myself seriously rooting for an athlete who was younger than I was. This doesn't sound like an experience that can seriously change you, and at the time, the age thing didn't really mean that much to me. But looking back, it was a key point in my development as an adult: before Andruw Jones blasted onto my Braves, I liked athletes because of their height or lack thereof, maybe a novelty mechanical issue or perhaps their excess weight, or because of some particular quirky skill they had mastered.

Andruw was the first player I liked because of his total inexperience. He was a blank slate, and I liked that he was ascribable, that I could assign him to be what I wanted him to be. What I wanted was for Andruw to be a power-hitting center fielder who could run like the wind and had an arm like a howitzer. And sure enough, as he revealed himself to Braves fans, I discovered he had all of these assets. Normally, a young athlete comes into a sports fan's life, and we generate the highest possible hopes for him, and then he eventually lets us down. Sometimes it happens immediately, sometimes over time, but a young athlete living up to our fullest expectations is as rare as a stand-up triple.

Andruw, though, he did it. Right from the start, he blasted home runs, tore up the basepaths, threw out runners at home, and dove headfirst to pluck balls out of the air just before they grazed the grass. He could do nothing wrong, and whenever he did screw up, we blamed it on his youth and expected him to learn from the mistake.

And then he'd smile. Or maybe it wasn't a smile but a smirk. Or a grimace. Whatever it was, Andruw's face always seemed to twist into an apologetic grin. This was endearing initially, but after a decade, seeing a guy strike out with two men on and then smile widely became harder to reconcile.

For his first few years in the majors, Andruw looked like he was about twelve years old. His legs seemed to reach to his neck, his eyes were open wide almost as if in wonderment, like he was as surprised by his dominance of the majors as we were. The moment Andruw went from being a dream to being human came midway through the 1998 season, when Andruw was all of twenty-one. After a fly ball dropped in front of him in center field, a ball that Andruw might have been able to catch had he been running full speed, Bobby Cox yanked him from the game, right then and there, during the middle of the inning. Short of Bobby getting on the PA system and cursing Andruw out, substituting for him in the middle of the inning was the most public way imaginable for Cox to show his displeasure with Andruw's laconic play. It was disrespectful and embarrassing. On purpose.

Just as my father taught me lessons without speaking them, Bobby did the same with Andruw. And in both situations, it worked. Meanwhile, we Braves fans had to take a side: was Bobby right to humiliate Andruw, or was Andruw correct to play the game with panache at the occasional expense of results? It was one of the first times we had been put in that position, where we had to decide whether to believe in Bobby or believe in one of his players. The fans seemed to choose Bobby, as did I. And Andruw chose Bobby, too—instead of pouting or spouting off in the media, Andruw came back the next night and played harder, and Cox repaid him with unabated loyalty from then on.

I n 2005, with four of the Braves' five starting pitchers hurt and Chipper Jones on the disabled list, Andruw suddenly put it all together. The Baby Braves took turns producing that season, but Andruw was rock steady: he hit 51 home runs and drove in 128 RBIs, both National League highs and both career highs for Andruw. He finished second in the MVP voting to Albert Pujols of St. Louis.

His stats began declining after that, and shortly before Andruw became a free agent in the winter of 2007, his agent, the legendarily money-hungry Scott Boras, announced that Andruw would be seeking a large, long contract. In almost a preemptive move, as soon as the season ended, the Braves announced they wouldn't be able to afford Andruw and wished him the best moving forward. The hot stove league proved chillier than usual, but Andruw ended up signing a two-year contract worth $36.2 million with the Los Angeles Dodgers.

Throughout his career, Andruw has had a fundamental inability to hit the baseball to right field. In interviews, Andruw says he doesn't hit the ball to right because he's simply a pull hitter, and he's more effective at yanking the ball to left field with power than trying to poke the ball to right field with finesse. This is his story, and he has stubbornly stuck to it, for over a decade now. I still remember watching a game against the San Diego Padres in 2004 when Andruw awkwardly reached out and obviously attempted to slap a pitch toward right field, and I was so shocked I nearly fell off my couch. This would happen about three or four times a season, and then Andruw would go back to trying to pull every pitch, missing and collapsing onto his left knee.

Either Andruw knew his strengths and did his best to play

within his skill set, or he's just an incomplete baseball player—the kind of player I didn't think he would turn out to be. He's a really good incomplete player, maybe the best incomplete player I've ever seen, but incomplete nonetheless. Despite uncovering the truth about Andruw, I supported him continuously, embracing his defense and the way he played the game, always with elegance and dynamism.

That night at Turner Field, as Andruw made himself at home in the batter's box, Edgar Renteria took a lead off second base.

"That's odd," I said.

"What?" Dad asked.

"You know how Andruw never hits the ball to right field?"

"Yeah."

"Look at Pittsburgh's center fielder, how he's shading Andruw to hit the ball to right." Maybe Andruw would try to advance the runner to third.

My dad didn't respond, though he looked suspiciously toward the outfield.

"Andruw's been hot, though," I said, clapping my hands together a few times to try generating some good luck for Andruw. "Maybe he'll pull one into that gap in left."

Three pitches later, Andruw reached out and poked a home run over the right-field wall, my dad cackling out loud as the ball soared exactly where I predicted it wouldn't go. So what do I know?

The Braves carried a four-run lead over the Pirates into the seventh inning that night, when Bobby Cox removed starting pitcher Chuck James. Dad and I had been monitoring James's pitch count and we knew he was hovering around 100, which is historically Cox's cue to turn to the bullpen. This always drives my dad crazy.

"You know," Dad will frequently rant, "back in the fifties and sixties, they didn't worry about things like pitch counts and bringing in all these relief pitchers. Nobody had ever heard of a pitch count back then!"

I usually point out that pitchers also weren't able to have 20-year careers back then because their managers were wearing them out by having them throw 150 pitches every fourth night. While I am generally not one to blindly embrace conventional wisdom, the concept of throwing fewer pitches and getting more out of the pitchers you've got so much money invested in seems to be full of logic.

On this night, Cox replaced James with Tyler Yates, a relief pitcher who spent the 2007 season retiring batters with fast pitches more so than with craft. During the weeks leading up to this game, Yates had earned a more prominent role with the team by upping his consistency: throwing more strikes, retiring more batters. It seemed Bobby was starting to trust him, and I was, too.

Yates entered and immediately got Xavier Nady to ground out to short, then walked a batter and gave up a solid single to right field. With two runners suddenly on base, I wondered aloud if Cox should at least send pitching coach Roger McDowell out to talk to Yates, to perhaps settle him down and remind him to stay within himself. Cox also had the option of pulling Yates and replacing him with Rafael Soriano, a flame-throwing reliever who had posted a great 2007 season thus far. Cox did not choose either of these options, instead believing that Yates would find his own way out of this trouble. By not making any move at that point—by staying silent—Cox had at the very least sent a message to Yates that he believed Yates would be able to get out of this trouble on his own; whether or not Bobby actually believed this is debatable.

Yates induced the next hitter, catcher Ronny Paulino, to chop a ball high off the plate and toward third base, where Chipper Jones waited about two days for it to drop from the murky sky and then unleashed a wild throw to first that skipped into foul territory, allowing a run to score and shrinking Atlanta's lead to 4–1. Dad and I agreed that Cox had made the right decision having Yates pitch to Paulino, because despite the run scoring, the reliever had basically done his job, getting the batter to hit a harmless ground ball to third; there was no way Cox could have predicted Chipper would throw the ball halfway to Chattanooga.

With two runners on and still only one out, Pittsburgh shortstop Jack Wilson came to the plate. Yates worked a two-strike count and then burned a fastball across the inside corner of the plate, surprising Wilson, for a strikeout. Two on, two out, and Yates had seemingly rediscovered his mojo, with the Pirates' weak-hitting pitcher due to bat next.

Manager Jim Tracy instead sent pinch-hitter Ryan Doumit to the plate, and as a light rain began to fall, Cox sprang from the dugout and shuffled toward the mound, his artificial knees seeming to creak with each step. "Leave him in, Cox!" my dad yelled, but we both knew Cox had no intention of allowing Yates to remain in the game. Cox rarely goes to the mound without removing his pitcher; if a pep talk or mechanical adjustment is needed, the task usually falls to McDowell; if someone has to be removed from the game, Bobby almost always handles that himself. Cox motioned down to the bullpen with a jiggle of his right arm, like he was about to roll dice, which in a way he was, and seconds later Rafael Soriano emerged through a door in the outfield wall. With his expressionless face and hat pulled down low on his brow in an intimidating manner, Soriano had been the Braves' most competent relief pitcher all season, so his appearance should have comforted us. Instead we sat there and tried to figure out why Cox wouldn't let Yates pitch to one more batter, especially since he'd just struck out the previous hitter, and save Soriano for the eighth inning, when he could enter fresh and face the top of the Pirates' batting order.

Of course, in the heat of the moment, Dad and I conveniently ignored any sort of advanced thinking on the matter, not pausing to consider that maybe Yates was tired or perhaps Soriano had done well in the past against Doumit. All we cared about was what we'd seen on the field. We were just scratching the surface of this conundrum when Soriano grooved a 3–2 fastball over the center of the plate. Within moments of the ball leaving Doumit's bat, Dad and I knew it was gone, both of us groaning as the initial arc and speed of the ball indicated that this was a definite home run. The ball eventually banged down into the seats in right-center. Tie game, 4–4.

"I told him he should've left Yates in," my dad muttered. I nodded my assent. He *had* told Bobby that. I'd heard it.

Soriano quickly recorded the third out, and then the skies opened and rain poured. The umpires waved all the players back to their respective dugouts, and the grounds crew sprinted out and unfurled a vast blue tarp that covered the infield, protecting the meticulously combed dirt and grass. We looked up into the night, trying to gauge the chances of the rain passing through, but we couldn't draw any conclusions. I texted a friend who had access to the internet and the current Doppler radar, and he said it looked like it was going to be a long delay. Dad and I decided to make a run for the car.

As I navigated my rental SUV back north up Peachtree Street, we listened to the broadcast on the radio, where Chip Caray and Joe Simpson were killing time during the rain delay by describing the actions of the grounds crew—"It looks like they're going to do a tarp dump into short right"—and taking calls from fans.

During the ride home, my dad and I began talking about handling my grandmother's will. Not five minutes outside Turner Field, and real life had returned to our lives. We have never had one of those relationships where we can talk comfortably about everyday problems, like dating or financial planning. Maybe it was a Baptist thing, or that Southern thing, or a Southern Baptist thing, but in our house delicate issues tended to be danced around rather than confronted head-on. I love my dad and my dad loves me; I know this and he knows this, and we both move on with our lives without feeling a need to actually say the words over and over. Our passive emotional connection made talking about my grandmother's death more difficult than it probably needed to be.

I had anticipated this, which is why I had scheduled us the session with Bobby. I knew Bobby was just about the only way we'd be able to get through the weekend. Just sitting there in silence during most of the game, not being forced to ponder death and instead being allowed to question and laugh about the game, this distracted us. And, in the end, it made us feel better. Dad and I never discussed this, but we both knew it was true. By not talking about things, we made them better.

But Bobby still should've left in Yates.

CHAPTER 9

PATIENCE: How Tom Glavine Is Like
Going on Safari in Africa

There are some athletes who are special to watch thanks to their sheer athletic supremacy. Watching Tom Glavine pitch, however, was sometimes about as compelling as watching your spouse solve a crossword puzzle. He always competed hard, with an appropriate amount of seriousness, but he did it with a certain concentration that was easily confused with joylessness or even a lack of passion. To be honest, Tom Glavine was often boring to watch. This was partly because of Glavine's physical gifts, which were not overt, though he maximized what he had; and it was partly because of his approach to pitching, which was mostly perfect.

Glavine threw mainly three or four pitches, though for the first few years he threw what seemed like just two: a fastball and a changeup. He nibbled and nibbled at the outside corner of the plate, aiming pitch after pitch as far away from the batter as he could while staying reasonably close to the strike zone, then only occasionally tempting fate by throwing perhaps one inside pitch per hitter. Almost everything he threw was within the eighty-mile-an-hour purview, which meant that even between the fastball and the changeup, his velocity didn't change much. Glavine really was Braves pitching coach Leo Mazzone's star pupil, the Brave who most exemplified Mazzone's theory that pitching down and away was the right way; that giving batters nothing to hit was the secret to success. And if there was something they could hit, make sure it was a pitch the batters couldn't do much with.

It wasn't a very dynamic plan of attack. Other pitchers challenged hitters and relished the machismo of the testosterone-fueled showdown—mano a mano, power against power. Glavine rarely overpowered anyone. With his average arm but precise control, Glavine basically *had* to accept Mazzone's passivity plan. It wasn't exciting, was never really all that interesting, but it worked, and Glavine rode it to over 300 career wins. Glavine's sustained success was a result of his constant sublimation of almost every urge to be aggressive.

Probably the most important thing about Tom Glavine was that he threw left-handed; this made him a perfect complement to Maddux and Smoltz, two of baseball's best right-handers, and forced teams in a three-game series to adjust to a right-left-right combination. In fact, if Glavine had thrown right-handed, he might not have even played baseball for a living. We were often told that had Glavine not been a baseball player, he could have been a professional hockey player. Glavine, who grew up in Massachusetts, hockey country, was actually a fourth-round 1984 NHL draft choice. Even though I've seen photos of Glavine in a hockey uniform, and he had hockey player hair for a few years early in his career, and I know for a fact that he was drafted by the L.A. Kings, I'm still not sure I believe Glavine as a hockey player. He was listed at six feet tall, 205 pounds, though even those numbers seem like an exaggeration. I always thought of hockey players as big, tough, toothless guys. To me, the notion of Tom Glavine playing hockey is about as believable as Bobby Cox participating in a dunk contest.

When asked why he chose baseball over hockey, Glavine told ESPN.com: "I guess after going through both sports and doing a pros and cons for both sports, they were both evenly matched in my mind. I love both sports, but the deciding factor was, being a left-handed pitcher, I had a huge advantage in baseball because of that, and I didn't have that type of advantage in hockey. I knew how desperately everyone wanted a left-handed pitcher, so it was an advantage that I needed to try and use."

I find that answer revealing. First, that Glavine, even as a teenager, actually had the presence of mind to sit down and work up a pros-and-cons list for his future. But second, that he was pragmatic enough to realize, even then, that being left-handed was such a huge advantage in baseball that it should be a deciding factor. Which isn't to say that Tom Glavine didn't love baseball more than he loved hockey or golf or shuffleboard or Ping-Pong; I don't know what Tom Glavine's heart told him to do. But his stoic approach to baseball regularly suggested to those of us watching that he didn't care as much—as much as the other players, or as much as we, the fans, cared. Glavine's stone face projected to fans that baseball was only a job. And a job he excelled at.

When baseball's players union went on strike in 1994, causing the cancellation of the World Series and the first loss of a postseason in ninety years, suddenly, there was Tom Glavine on the news every night. As the Braves' representative to the Major League Baseball players union, and as a member of the union's executive committee, Glavine, along with pitcher David Cone of the Kansas City Royals, became one of the public faces of the striking players, doing seemingly endless interviews to explain why the players making millions just weren't being given every advantage. All we knew, as Braves fans, was that the team we'd waited for so long to become a contender had been taken away from us, and no amount of rationalizing at press conferences by one of our starting pitchers was going to curb that frustration.

This seems as good a time as any to note that when the strike hit on August 12, 1994, the Braves were in second place in the NL East, six games behind the Montreal Expos. Because the season never *officially* ended, the Braves never *officially* lost the division. And if the season had ended, the Braves were leading the race for the NL wild card—a rule instituted just that year—so they still would have qualified for the postseason. They'd won three division titles in a row, and then after the strike, the next year, 1995, they went right back to winning the division, and they won eleven more division titles in a row. So even though they didn't actually win the NL East title in 1994, neither did anyone else. The way I see it, the Braves won fourteen division titles in a row. Occasionally fans of other teams will bring up the fact that the Braves didn't *really* win the division for fourteen years in a row. Which, if we're dealing in semantics, is true. But the Braves *did* win fourteen division titles in a row. If you ask me.

One fall afternoon, not long after our epic trip out West, Nana Carolyn died after a massive heart attack. Paw Paw lived another two decades before he passed in 2008 at the age of ninety-three. When Paw Paw died, all the grandkids were asked what, if anything, we wanted from his home to remember him by. I asked for a map that he had hanging inside the house on his farm. After every trip, my grandfather used a black marker and traced each trip's route on this map. It's beaten up and frayed around the edges—he Scotch-taped it to the wood paneling in his house—but I had it framed and convinced my wife that it belongs over the couch in our apartment. Seeing it every day not only reminds me of Paw Paw but also reinforces the importance he put on expanding horizons, seeing places you've never seen, appreciating the diversity of the world in which we live.

Largely because of Paw Paw, the thing I became most passionate about as an adult—besides the Braves—has been traveling. Isabel and I have been from Hawaii to Barcelona, from Paris to Rio de Janeiro. The catch when it comes to traveling is that as much as I've enjoyed seeing the world, I hate being away from New York for more than a week at a time. I like to travel, but I also like to work. I love what I do for a living, and for many years it seemed as though the more frequently I wrote, the more value I had in my field. I clawed and scratched to make a name for myself, and I was afraid to take a breather for fear of losing my grip on this life I've created for myself. I still remember arriving on a tiny Caribbean island for our honeymoon and discovering that Kobe Bryant had been arrested in Colorado, then running to find a computer with internet access so I could update my blog with all the most relevant news stories I could find. So it's always been a constant struggle to find a workable balance between getting away but not being away for too long.

Isabel pushed me for years to take a long trip, to forget everything for a while. I thought of how even Bobby occasionally gives Braves players a day off to keep their minds fresh. So we dipped into our savings, took time off work, and made plans to experience Africa. We had to get so many shots before we left, for so many ancient diseases, that I told Isabel I wondered if we were going to Africa or if we were traveling back in time. As it turned out, in many ways, we were doing both.

As our propeller plane taxied to a halt on the dirt runway in Laikipia, in central Kenya, I noticed three native guys hanging around an open-backed Land Rover. I hoped they were there to meet us, because they were the only humans around as far as I could see. Their bodies were wrapped with vibrant fabrics, their legs and arms and necks accented with dozens of decorative beads.

These were our hosts. Their names were Lemarti, Boniface, and Mex. Boniface was the joker of the three, always smiling, with a loud laugh like a hyena. Mex didn't speak much English, so he was mostly quiet; his hair had been dyed a bright magenta and braided into long, thin strands that hung down to his elbows. A few colorful feathers and plastic flowers were woven into the top of his hair, giving him an extra foot of height. Lemarti was the leader of the group and the namesake of the campground where we were staying. Lemarti grew up in the region, a member of the Samburu tribe, before meeting and marrying Kenyan fashion designer Anna Trzebinski in 2002. Together they set up a luxurious tourist camp along a bend on the Ewaso River, in the cool shade of a majestic fig tree. All three of the guys waiting for us had grown up in rural villages and completed various rites of passage to qualify them as warriors, from branding their stomachs to killing wild animals. They'd be taking care of us for the next few days. They set aside their spears and holstered their machetes in order to take our bags from the plane's pilot.

After a ninety-minute ride through the sunburned, arid land, we arrived at Lemarti's Camp, a verdant patch of grass that stood out as if set against the surface of Mars. Lemarti's Camp was staffed by about a dozen Samburu warriors, friends of Lemarti's, and they took care of everything at the camp, from cooking to cleaning. The camp itself was essentially a series of huge tents decorated with an eye toward sumptuousness—overstuffed couches, a dinner table made from beached wood, a makeshift bar area—all atop raised, rich hardwood flooring. The tent Isabel and I would sleep in had a king-sized bed surrounded by mosquito netting, fronted by a deck that hung twenty feet above the Ewaso.

I woke up early each morning to find waiting outside our tent a French press of Kenyan coffee and a thermos of steaming water, accompanied by a basket of warm macadamia muffins. I spent hours sitting there every morning before Isabel was awake, drinking my coffee, watching a family of gazelles playing on the hill across the river in the light of the rising sun, letting thoughts dance in my head. I'd forgotten what it was like to really think, to sit back and give thoughts and problems the time to percolate and work themselves out. I spent a lot of time at Lemarti's doing nothing, just sitting around and watching the river run, listening to the wild birds sing, processing the scent of the acrid dirt—the smell of which reminded me over and over again of Paw Paw's farm back in Alabama. Late at night, when it turned cool, we sat around a campfire with the warriors, under an endless sky bursting with stars. When everyone went to sleep, the silence was almost too loud for me to be comfortable.

The baseball strike dragged into 1995. President Bill Clinton got involved in January, forcing the two sides to resume negotiations, but a settlement wasn't reached until March. As grateful as everyone was that the strike was over, fans all over the country were still bitter—a fan in Cincinnati hired a plane to fly over the field on opening day with a sign that read "Owners & Players: To hell with all of you!"

As the public face of the union, Tom Glavine was booed on opening night in Atlanta, and then booed for weeks whenever he took the mound. While fans around baseball protested by neither watching nor attending games, fans in Atlanta came back sooner than most. We were still in the honeymoon phase of our relationship with these winning Braves. We knew that elusive World Series win had to be somewhere right around the corner.

The Braves made it to the series again that year, and while David Justice's huge home run gave Atlanta the lead in the deciding game six of the 1995 World Series, Glavine started and pitched a nearly perfect game—the game of his life. He limited the Indians to one hit and three walks over eight innings, throwing dozens of changeups on the outside corner as the Braves won 1–0. According to *Sports Illustrated,* the game was scoreless in the middle of the fifth when Glavine ran into the dugout and said,

"C'mon! Let's get a run! Because I know they sure as hell aren't getting any." That kind of fiery leadership from Glavine seems nearly unimaginable. It doesn't jibe with the image Glavine seemed to persistently project, and in the *SI* story, Cox and Leo Mazzone were both surprised by Glavine's outburst, too.

Glavine might not have been able to beat you with his athleticism, but he could definitely wear you down. I attended numerous Braves games throughout the nineties, and because the Braves used a five-man pitching rotation, I always had a 1-in-5 chance of going to a game on a night when Tom Glavine would be pitching. Looking at it differently, you could say I had a 4-in-5 chance of going on a night when Tom Glavine would *not* be pitching; I could be seeing Maddux or Smoltz or Mercker or Avery or whomever. But for reasons that remain unclear to me, I *always* seemed to go to Braves games when Tom Glavine was starting. I couldn't afford season tickets, so I generally went with a friend at the last minute and bought the cheapest tickets available and then sat in the best empty seats we could find. More times than I can recall, I walked into Turner Field and heard, "And on the mound for the Braves, number forty-seven . . ." To this day, family and friends still ask me if Glavine is starting when I tell them I'm attending a Braves game, even though he retired in 2009.

You might think that getting to see a 300-game winner pitch in person so often was a privilege. And it was, the first dozen times. I didn't care that Glavine had been the face of the strike. Watching someone try to induce his opponent to give up isn't thrilling spectacle. Maddux was already the greatest savvy pitcher in baseball, and while Smoltz had power, he usually relied on a wicked slider to get outs. Glavine, meanwhile, nibbled and nibbled and nibbled away. If a man got on base, Glavine threw to first so many times that even the home fans started grumbling.

In the winter of 2002–03, with the Braves' nineties core evaporating, Tom Glavine signed a contract to play for our archrivals, the New York Mets. Glavine inked a three-year deal that reportedly would be worth $35 million, with an option for a fourth season that could kick in based on the number of innings Glavine pitched, which could raise the value of the contract to $42.5 million. "It's almost surreal that it happened," Glavine told the Associated Press upon signing with the Mets. "I never thought I would play for someone else. I thought I would play my whole career with the Braves. I held out hope that things would work out, but they didn't. There's a lot of emotions. It's a tough time."

The Braves replaced Glavine with a cheaper option in Russ Ortiz, who went 21–7 with a 3.81 ERA. In New York, during his first season, 2003, Glavine went 9–14 with a 4.52 ERA.

I'd moved to Manhattan a few years before Glavine, and I found it amusing to see Mets fans do a 180 upon learning they'd signed this formerly hated rival. The guy who they'd previously called too much of a wimp to challenge his opponents was suddenly hailed as a crafty left-hander, a steady vet, a pitcher who kept his wits about him no matter what. Mets fans had mostly positive reactions about getting a pitcher of Glavine's caliber, particularly one they were poaching from the Braves, and seeing a buzz of energy as the Mets married Glavine was strange to me; I'd been lulled into a comfortable numbness through the years by his peaceful pitching, and I realized it had been difficult for me to appreciate his value to the Braves.

Glavine struggled in New York, and he didn't finish a season over .500 until the final year of his contract, when it was about to expire. In that 2006 season—the extra year of the contract the Braves had refused to offer him—Glavine went an impressive 15–7 and re-signed with the Mets for the 2007 season. On the final day of the 2007 season, with the Mets desperately needing a win over the Marlins to have a chance at making the postseason, Glavine started the crucial game and pitched what had to be the worst game of his life. After walking the leadoff batter and getting a force-out from the second hitter, Glavine gave up a single, a single, a double, a single, a walk, a single, and then he hit a batter. In total, Glavine faced nine hitters, recorded one out, gave up five hits, two walks, and seven earned runs.

In 2008 Glavine re-signed with the Braves. He spent most of the year on the disabled list and won two games, and then, in June 2009, after Glavine had made a few rehab starts in the minor leagues and was eligible to return to the majors, the Braves released him. Glavine held out hope of pitching with another team, but no other teams shared Glavine's faith. He never pitched in the majors again.

Some day in the near future, Tom Glavine is going to be elected to the National Baseball Hall of Fame. Between 1991 and 2002, Glavine never had a losing season, he is one of only six left-handed pitchers in baseball history to reach 300 wins, and his two Cy Young Awards and ten trips to the All-Star Game make his eventual appointment to Cooperstown all but certain. Tom Glavine may never have had the gas to throw fastballs past hitters, but he had the patience to grind down everyone he faced.

———————————

One evening Lemarti took us out for a drive. Isabel and I piled in the back of the truck alongside Boni and Mex, while Lemarti, Anna, and their young daughter sat up front. We bumped through the desiccated bushes and trees, spotting gazelles and dik-diks every few feet. Twenty minutes in, Lemarti, Mex, and Boni fell silent and then started whispering in Maa, their indigenous language, and then Mex hopped out of the truck and ran ahead of us, sprinting back occasionally to consult with Lemarti and suggest a different route. Finally, I asked what was happening, and Boni leaned forward and whispered that we were tracking a herd of wild elephants.

A moment later, we squeezed between two bushes and popped into a clearing to discover six or seven elephants eating leaves from trees. Lemarti killed the engine, and the truck rolled to a halt, maybe twenty feet away from the largest animals I'd ever seen in person. Nobody said a word; the only sound was that of elephants snapping off limbs and chewing. Suddenly the biggest elephant, which must have stood at least twelve feet tall, turned to face us. I felt as though it was looking me in the eyes. The wind inflated its ears out like balloons, making it seem more menacing than it probably actually was. Isabel whispered that we were too close, and I felt a shiver of terror run through my bones. With maybe five steps, that elephant could have been on top of us. I looked into the cab of the truck and observed Lemarti sitting there, holding his young daughter, and I felt reassured, knowing we must have been safe because Lemarti wouldn't put his young child in danger. Then again, they were in the cab, and we were in the back of the open-air truck. Maybe ten seconds later, the elephant lazily turned and went back to eating its dinner. And Isabel and I exhaled.

Our first night at Lemarti's, I woke around two in the morning after hearing some undetermined sound from near the river outside our tent. It wasn't a growl or a roar or a bark or a squawk; it was more like a *whoosh* sound. I was instantly wide awake. Even though we were surrounded by actual warriors, men who hunted and killed every day in order to provide for and protect their families, and who had promised to protect us, some internal instinct told me to be scared.

I held my breath and listened carefully, then nearly jumped through the roof of the tent when Isabel suddenly asked, "Did you hear that?" It, the noise, whatever it was, had awoken her too. We lay there in silence and heard it again. *Whoosh.* It was the sound of water being swept aside. *Whoosh. Whoosh.* Was somebody wading through the river? The warriors had told us that several of them would stay up all night and patrol the camp, just in case some wild animal wandered along. Were they hearing this noise?

The *whooshes* started to dissipate, and I lay there for a while until, mercifully, I was the victim of only jet lag. Hours later I woke with the sun and had my coffee, then wandered over to the main tent, where Lemarti and Mex were awake and engrossed in some sort of indigenous board game that resembled back-gammon. A warrior handed me a warm mug of freshly brewed chai masala tea.

"Good morning, Lang!" Lemarti called cheerily. "Did you sleep well last night?"

"Funny you should ask," I said. As I spooned fresh honey into my tea, I described the sound we'd heard and asked Lemarti and Mex if they'd heard anything. They not only hadn't heard anything, they didn't seem the least bit alarmed. "If it was in the water, it probably was a fish," Lemarti reasoned. Did the Ewaso harbor mermaids, I wondered? Boniface came bopping in a few minutes later, and to my relief, he had heard the *whoosh*. He laughed as I told him how nervous Isabel and I had been and assured me that we were as safe as could be. He agreed with Lemarti that it was probably just a fish.

That night, we heard it again. I wanted to start screaming for someone to come and check and see what it was, but Boniface had succeeded in calming my fears, at least minimally. The next morning over breakfast, Boni told us that one of the warriors had gone down to investigate the sound and discovered an enormous catfish stuck in the shallow water against the bank of the river, thrashing to and fro. *Whoosh. Whoosh.* Even though we were roughly seven thousand miles from Paw Paw's farm in Alabama, the same fish that lived an unassuming life there was able to scare me within a breath of my life in Kenya.

Our final morning at Lemarti's, we woke, packed, and ambled over to the main tent for breakfast. Lemarti, we were told, wasn't around, because overnight there had been a gunshot heard from somewhere far across the river, from someone who wasn't supposed to be there, and Lemarti and a few of the guys had been chasing this unidentified hunter down all night to make sure he knew he was on their land and was not welcome. I understand this sounds a little crazy, but upon being told this news I just nodded and had another bite of cereal. I thought back and realized that I actually *had* heard a loud bang in the middle of the night, but I'd somehow managed not to be alarmed and had gone right back to sleep. I never thought I'd be at a point in my life where I'd sleep through gunshots, but here

I was in the African bush, sleeping through gunshots. There's a certain unpredictability to life in Africa out in the bush, and we had no choice but to embrace it.

Hanging around with Lemarti and Boni for a week, I was impressed by their relentless fearlessness. It was a part of them, something innate. We spend so much time afraid of the future, fearful of things we may or may not even need to face. But these guys just go. They don't seem to be afraid—ever—not just of life but of anything.

After our final breakfast in Laikipia, I grabbed a cup of chai masala and took a seat on our deck, looking out at the river. It was quiet out, except for the burbling water. The sun was starting to soar in the sky, the monkeys across the way emerging from slumber. We spent almost ten days in Africa, enough time for me to forget about the Braves' West Coast road trip and the impending NBA free agency period. By finally allowing myself to be patient with an experience, I was rewarded with one of the greatest trips of my life. I felt like I'd found myself, thousands of miles from home.

B obby Cox's first stint as manager of the Atlanta Braves was from 1978 until 1981. In '81, the Braves finished fifth and Ted Turner fired Cox. At the press conference announcing the firing, Turner was asked who his replacement would be. "It would be Bobby Cox if I hadn't just fired him," the owner said. "We need someone like him around here."

Bobby was immediately hired as manager by the Toronto Blue Jays. Before Bobby moved north of the border, the Jays had finished in last place in each of their five seasons of existence. Cox came in and by his fourth season led the Blue Jays to the AL East pennant and the playoffs.

And then he left and returned to Atlanta as the general manager of the Braves. It turned out that the guy Ted Turner needed wasn't someone *like* Bobby Cox, it was Bobby himself. Cox had to return to Atlanta to become one of the greatest managers in the history of baseball. Ted Turner offered him a five-year deal worth $1.8 million to run the team's front office. At the conference announcing his return to Atlanta, Cox said, "I won't miss the dirt, the dirty uniforms, arguing with umpires and the fines . . . [Toronto] treated me as good as a manager can be treated. I live just twenty miles north of the [Braves'] ball-park, and that was the biggest factor."

If Cox had never managed another baseball game, his record would have been 621–615, a wash. And the plan for Cox was not to manage again: he was supposed to guide the development of the organization and pick the managers. He could have gone down in history as just another manager, one who made the postseason once but, on the whole, was pretty even. But things didn't work out with the manager Bobby had hired, Russ Nixon, and Bobby had to slip back into uniform. The rest is his story, and history.

One of Bobby's greatest strengths has continuously been his patience; he always gives his players every chance to be successful; no Braves player can say he didn't have a chance to prove himself to Bobby. Sometimes this means he gives them too many chances to fail, or he waits too long to conclude the guy can't do the job he's been asked to do. Either way, when Bobby's patience is rewarded, it's gratifying, not only for the club but also for us fans to see a player put it all together. How many guys on other teams never got that opportunity because who-ever was in charge didn't have the patience to allow them to fully realize their abilities?

I'm all for seizing the day and taking command of your own destiny, but I also believe that sometimes having the patience to allow yourself to be patient can be the most rewarding gift of all.

CHAPTER 10

HOPE: How Jason Heyward Is Like Starting a Family

When I was growing up, every winter, once the Falcons were done disappointing Atlanta sports fans and the Celtics, Bulls, and/or Pistons had symbolically shamed the Hawks out of the NBA title chase, the Braves would begin spring training in West Palm Beach, Florida. West Palm, as it was often referred to, is about seventy miles from Miami, up Florida's eastern seaboard. The Braves encamped there each March from 1963 through 1997, regular as clockwork. I'd been to Disney World and to the Florida Panhandle on family vacations, but my only real exposure to West Palm Beach came from the occasional radio broadcasts of the rehearsal games on WSB-AM 750 in Atlanta. Games I listened to on the radio usually revealed teams playing with gap-toothed rosters, taking care to rest any regular players nursing even the slightest tweak or muscle pull while sparingly using the pitchers anyone had actually heard of. The results of spring training games are not in the scores but in the development and observation of the players.

I always imagined West Palm Beach as a film noir locale, the games played in sepia tones under a boiling sun, everyone constantly soaking wet from the oppressive humidity, fans sitting in folding beach chairs in the shade of palm trees sipping on iced hard liquor in short glasses, wearing tank tops and straw hats, speaking in quiet tones, the air in the dugouts stirred only occasionally by a few laconic ceiling fans. And I'm going to assume that's how it was. In 1998, the Braves moved from West Palm Beach, where they shared their training facility with the Expos, north to Orlando. More specifically, the Braves moved directly into Walt Disney World, of all places. I later learned that they moved north in part because the climate; West Palm Beach actually was the pressure cooker of my dreams. More important, by moving to Orlando, not only did the Braves get an entire brand-new baseball complex to themselves but—and I'm guessing this was the reason for anyone in the Braves organization who cared about buzz and corporate synergy—the Braves were suddenly an official part of Disney, Inc. And with hordes of tourists wandering around each spring, escaping their suburban existences to a Disney-vetted version of fun, the Braves would probably be beneficiaries of weary families or even baseball fans who'd exhausted their options in the amusement parks and had a few hours to kill, and disposable dollars to spend on hats and shirts and collectibles.

The last week of March 2009, I stepped off a flight from New York City and into Orlando International Airport—my first visit to spring training. The terminal was bright and airy, with palm trees lining the paths of the trams that carry travelers from terminal to terminal. The airport was jammed with exhausted-looking families, coming or going to or from the vacation of a lifetime, almost all of them battling some shade of profound sunburn.

Once I navigated past the tourists, I set my rental car GPS toward Champion Stadium.

Even though Champion Stadium was nearly a decade old, it appeared brand new from the outside. I suppose that's the Disney showbiz effect—managing appearances, keeping everything shiny and new at least on the outermost layer. The exterior of the stadium was painted a lemony color and featured Spanish flourishes, as though it had been designed by De Soto just after he found the fountain of youth over in St. Augustine.

I arrived a few innings into the game, picked up my media credential, and as I settled into my seat in the press box, I learned that new Braves signee Kenshin Kawakami had been scratched from his start that evening. No Braves fans except maybe for those in Japan had heard of Kawakami before he'd been signed. Yet, with the Braves desperate for pitching and Kawakami interested in testing his skills in America, the two struck a deal, and suddenly one of our biggest off-season signings was a thirty-three-year-old Japanese pitcher with a history of arm problems.

The Braves were having a great spring—13–3 before my arrival—and that was mostly without key players such as Chipper Jones and Brian McCann, who had missed significant time while representing the United States in the World Baseball Classic. For a team whose pitchers had been poor a year earlier, the rebuilt pitching staff had allowed a Grapefruit League–low 56 runs; the Washington Nationals were a distant second with 83. Seeing a stat like that gave me immediate hope for the upcoming season.

The game ticked along at a brisk pace with many positive signs: Javy Vazquez started and was terrific, throwing 79 pitches, 52 for strikes; Jeff Bennett came on in relief and got out of a bases-loaded mess; Jeff Francoeur got a hit to the opposite field; our new backup catcher, David Ross, singled and drove in a run.

When the game ended, Mark Bowman and David O'Brien, the Braves' beat writers for MLB.com and the *Atlanta Journal-Constitution,* respectively, headed down to Cox's office. I followed the two of them down four flights of stairs to the clubhouse, and we stood and waited outside Cox's office. I introduced myself, and as O'Brien was pumping my hand, Cox appeared out of nowhere and ushered us all into his office.

It was a small room, maybe ten feet by ten feet. The walls were the color of a legal pad, a hue designed to be inoffensive to the widest possible swath of people. The office contained a small refrigerator filled with bottled water, and a single locker stall against the back wall. The other side of the room featured a small, dark brown desk with a matching credenza behind it; they looked as though they were purchased together on sale at Staples. There were a few stacks of paper on the desk, a pair of sunglasses resting upside down, and a telephone. No computer was in sight. Behind the desk on the credenza were a few cardboard boxes and two boxes of Macanudo cigars. A bulletin board on the wall had nine sheets of paper tacked neatly to it, most with Braves logos on the top. Some appeared to be schedules, some press releases. Two office chairs faced the desk and a small black couch was against the wall alongside the desk.

I stepped into the office just as Bobby slipped off his white Braves uniform pants. Baseball uniforms are composed of layers—the undershirt, sliding shorts, stirrups, jerseys, and so on—

and when I met him, Cox was somewhere in between all these different layers, like an unraveling onion. He had on a gray Braves-logo undershirt with blue sleeves, white compression shorts, and white socks covered by blue stirrups, pulled up just below his knees. About eight inches of skin was visible on each knee, and on each knee the skin was crisscrossed by jagged scars. He was a little shorter than I imagined, a little rounder than I expected. His hair was buzzed short, more salt than pepper.

Bobby plopped down in a rolling chair behind the desk, sighed, and said, "Yeah . . . crap." Only he didn't say "crap," he used a more descriptive word. The Braves had won 5–2, making them 14–3 in spring training. But it was late and Cox looked tired. A box score from the game was sitting on his desk, awaiting his arrival. Cox picked it up and stared hard at it. O'Brien started throwing out stats at Cox, and Cox responded with short answers, nothing more than five or six words at a time. When O'Brien mentioned that Matt Diaz had gone 2–3, Cox blurted, "Diaz is hitting about .400."

After a few minutes of chatter, Cox yawned, signaling the end of the session. It was nearing ten at night and the Braves had another game the next day at one. O'Brien and Bowman got up to leave. As they left, I took a step closer to Cox.

"Bobby," I said, "just wanted to introduce myself. My name is Lang Whitaker."

"Hey," Cox said, extending his hand and grasping mine, making eye contact. "Good to meet you."

"I'm actually here because I'm working on a book about being a Braves fan, about growing up a Braves fan."

"Well," he said, as he reached down to remove his right sock, "I'll do what I can to help you."

"Thanks, Bobby, I appreciate it."

Even though my professional career has placed me in a litany of remarkable situations with famous people—I've done everything from having a drink with Michael Jordan to interviewing Jimmy Carter to eating lunch with David and Victoria Beckham—I noticed that I was nervous, really nervous. The words I intended to speak to Bobby seemed to have no interest in leaving my mouth. "I, I mean, um, IgrewupinAtlanta andI'vealwaysrootedfortheBraves," I stammered. "The Braves are my favorite team. I live in New York now but I'm working on a book about being a Braves fan." Yes, I'd said the same thing a few sentences before.

"New York?" Cox asked, perking up a bit. "What do you do in New York?"

"I'm actually an editor at a basketball magazine, a magazine called *SLAM*. But baseball's always been one of my favorite sports."

"OK, well, good to meet you." Time for me to leave, Bobby said without saying.

"You too, Bobby. Really good to finally meet you."

Spring training is actually supposed to be a morning ritual. Aside from the occasional evening game—such as the one I'd attended the previous night—most mornings the players arrive with the sun. They work out, play a game, and are finished by early afternoon, with the evening to themselves.

On Saturday morning, by nine o'clock, I was threading my way through Disney traffic, windows down, OutKast in the CD player. I walked into the clubhouse a little before ten, and most of the Braves players were already there. Jorge Campillo had just returned from pitching for Mexico in the WBC and was trying to earn a spot in the Braves starting rotation. Jo-Jo Reyes asked him if Mexico pitching coach Fernando Valenzuela had tried to teach him a screwball. Campillo said he had, but added he, Campillo, hadn't mastered the pitch. He came over and showed Reyes the screwball grip, which seemed unbelievably complex, like his fingers were afflicted with a painful case of arthritis. Reyes proudly told Campillo that he'd almost hit a home run a few days earlier in a game in Clearwater.

For a franchise that has largely defined excellence over the past two decades, the clubhouse was a mostly generic space. There were no motivational slogans on the wall, no huge team logos embedded in the carpet. The clubhouse screamed temporary, like this was just a quick stop along the road to the games that actually mattered. Since it was toward the end of spring training, the lockers weren't fully populated, as everyone would be moving north in a couple of weeks and many of the minor league prospects had already been jettisoned from the big league camp. Even the lockers that were in use were mostly empty, filled with clothes and equipment. The only photo I saw in any locker was in the locker of Rafael Soriano, who had tacked to the side a picture of himself pitching.

I left the clubhouse, went down a hallway under the stands covered by a rubberized floor, down a ramp, and out into the dugout. Before me was that vast expanse of emerald grass. It looked amazing, like something out of a movie, perfectly tended and trimmed. Considering the field I'd played on in high school was covered with more dirt than grass, this was a real field of dreams.

I took a seat atop the bench toward first base. There were a few stacks of towels emblazoned with the Powerade logo along the top of the bench and a couple of baseballs lying around on the bench. Leaning on the steps to the field was one black bat (a Louisville Slugger M9 Powerized model), the name KYLE DAVIES burned into it. Davies, a starting pitcher, had been traded to Kansas City two years before; apparently he left a few bats behind.

The sun shone directly on me, but the roof of the dugout hid my face and arms, providing me a clear view of the outfield, where the entire Braves team was doing stretching exercises. The stands were empty and various songs from the seventies, eighties, and nineties played over the PA system, including a studiously comprehensive collection of the greatest hits of Hall & Oates.

A few more writers and an equipment manager filtered into the dugout and took seats, staring blankly out onto the field just as I was doing. There is something to be said for the soothing presence of a perfectly manicured baseball diamond. The massive hands on the scoreboard clock indicated it was exactly 10:25 a.m. when Bobby Cox emerged from the tunnel in full uniform and took a seat near where he usually sits during games, at the end of the dugout closest to home plate. I went down and sat near him. Michael Jackson's "Pretty Young Thing" came on over the PA system.

Out on the field, the Braves players paired off and started tossing baseballs back and forth, the horsehide pounding leather rhythmically, like popcorn popping. Bobby looked on occasionally, never seeming to focus on any one player in particular. I was hoping to use this time to pepper Bobby with everything I ever wanted to ask him, but Bobby had other plans. For the next twenty minutes, with Bobby at the helm, conversation in the dugout careened wildly, from workers' unions to Brian McCann's exceptional hitting ability to the stomach flu. Cox did not dominate the talk, but rather participated judiciously, turning his head, listening when other people spoke, even asking some follow-up questions.

Bobby was wearing a pair of newly shined black Mizuno cleats, which were untied. He leaned over to tie them. "Bobby," I said, "I heard you're the only manager in the majors who still wears metal spikes." I had read that somewhere a few years ago and have always loved that detail. Cox was clinging to tradition.

Cox answered, "Well . . . I don't know about that." He finished tying the right shoe and shifted to the left, closer to me.

"I think that's true," I said. Ever since reading that I'd informally checked the footwear of managers around Major League Baseball and hadn't seen any other guys in cleats. "Most of the managers wear running shoes now, right?" They preferred comfort over tradition.

"Yeah," he said. There was about a two-second pause as he finished tying his left shoe and pulled himself back upright.

And then he said, "I don't know . . . I just . . . I like 'em."

Soon after, the Mets players arrived at the park and drifted out onto the field to warm up. A batting cage materialized over home plate and as the Braves players took their turns in the cage, Cox ambled out to watch them hit and chat with the coaches. Batting practice was accompanied by the consistent sound of *thwack!* as balls were sprayed all over the field. I was standing a few feet behind home plate, chatting with Braves' strength and conditioning coach Phil Falco, when the *thwacks* were suddenly replaced by a series of *THWACKS!* It was as if someone inside the cage had cranked up the volume to eleven.

I turned and saw a tall, left-handed hitter in the cage wearing number 77. I wasn't sure who this was until I read the nameplate on the back of his jersey: HEYWARD. These deafening hits were coming from Jason Heyward, the Braves' highest-rated minor league outfield prospect. A few weeks later, Yahoo.com's Gordon Edes wrote a column about Heyward and quoted an anonymous major league scout who called Heyward "the best young hitter I've seen in years. He'll be leading the league in home runs for ten years once he gets here."

Though I'd turned up in Orlando wanting to get to know what Bobby Cox was like, a few hours after seeing batting practice up close, I left in my Oldsmobuick driving south on the Florida turnpike, thinking mostly about Jason Heyward. Bobby was pretty much exactly what I suspected he'd be like, but the surprise came from Jason Heyward. Part of being a fan of a sports team is accepting the responsibility of embracing not only results but also promise, with equal zeal. One does not exist without the other, and while the current numbers and headlines are how we stay tuned in, the promise of future production always gives us, the fans, hope. And that's a currency that never fluctuates in value.

The 2009 Braves season wasn't very memorable. They were four games under .500 heading into July, then turned some imaginary corner and were red-hot in the second half, finishing the year with a 60–36 run, to end the season 86–76 overall. This was good, above-average, but there weren't many inspirational moments, at least not in comparison to what we'd seen during previous pennant chases, most recently in 2005. The Braves finished the 2009 season third in their division and fourth in the National League Wild Card standings.

Maybe the most memorable moment of the 2009 season came at the end of September. While the Braves were in New York to play the Mets, Bobby Cox announced that the 2010 season would be his last as Braves manager. "If I don't do this right now, I would be wanting to manage again somewhere . . . or here," Bobby said. "It's time to go ahead and say it. I don't think I would ever give up the idea of managing unless I just say, 'That's it.' That's what I'm saying—that it's it."

The idea of Bobby Cox leaving the Braves was almost unfathomable—"I'll believe it when I see it," said Chipper Jones—but all of a sudden it was happening, and it was real. Two consecutive decades of Bobby Cox standing at the end of the dugout and shouting encouragement to the Braves now had an expiration date stamped on the side.

When spring training rolled around in 2010, everyone noted that it was Bobby's final spring training as a Brave, but the story that energized Braves fans was the rise of Jason Heyward. After I'd seen him crunching balls in the 2009 spring training, Heyward spent the rest of the year burning through Atlanta's minor league system, working his way from A-ball all the way to AAA, and was named the minor league player of the year by *USA Today* and *Baseball America*.

Heyward had a remarkable spring training in 2010, and each amazing feat—such as when he hit a home run into a parking lot and shattered a car's sun roof—was chronicled instantaneously via various forms of social media. For a Braves fan, it was like seeing the Bible being written in real time. Still just twenty years old, Heyward was hitting balls so hard and so far that the Braves had to erect a fence around an employee parking lot that had previously been thought of as unreachable by mere mortals, or at least by most Braves. As Bobby Cox was quoted regarding Heyward in a *New Yorker* story about spring training, "There are just some guys that hit the thing, and it's, like, *Oooh,* that's different. That's *way* different." Just when the hype seemed to reach a fever pitch, the season began and Heyward was given the starting job in right field. And as if to validate all the propaganda, on opening day, in his first major league at bat, Heyward drilled a 475-foot three-run homer into the right-field seats at Turner Field.

It felt a little magical, the notion of a twenty-year-old leading us into a new decade. And in Bobby's final season, I was willing to accept magic from wherever we could get it.

The Braves made several key changes in the months leading into the 2010 season. Most noticeably, the bullpen got a major overhaul, as young but inconsistent stoppers Rafael Soriano and Mike Gonzalez were replaced by a thirty-eight-year-old closer (Billy Wagner) and a forty-year-old set-up man (Takashi Saito). With Adam LaRoche gone, the Braves were needy at first base, so Troy Glaus was signed, a career third baseman they hoped to convert to first, who'd missed most of 2009 with a bum shoulder.

As the Braves were trying to figure out their future, I was considering mine, too. Isabel and I had married in 2003, and after a few days of wedded bliss, she started talking about wanting to have children. I countered this by making the calculated yet hopefully untraceable suggestion that we get a dog. Which we did and which, at least temporarily, bought me some time. Because here was what I knew: I was still in my twenties, and I wasn't ready to be a father, emotionally or financially. In retrospect, I realize that I probably shouldn't have worried back then. I know enough people of various ages and means who've had kids, and they all seem to have turned out fine; I guess you figure it out as you go. But I didn't understand this at the time, so our dog, Starbury, was partially a distraction for my own fear. A cute and cuddly distraction, but a distraction.

Once I finally got the guts to go for it and we began a concerted effort to have a child, life struck back. In February 2008, Isabel's mother suffered a fatal heart attack. Gone, just like that. A couple of months later, Paw Paw, who was ninety-three years old, sat down to eat breakfast at his farm one morning and never got up again. And then several months after that, my wife's brother died of a heart attack, a few months shy of his fifty-third birthday. You blink your eyes, and suddenly three of the most important people in your life just aren't there anymore. Three people we had always counted on for support, for a laugh, for unconditional love, had been yanked away from us, one after another after another, like someone systematically kicking the legs out from under your chair. And it left us both reeling.

By the time we found our footing and were ready to commit to starting a family, the doctors told us we were probably too late. As a garbage can full of negative pregnancy tests attested, we were too old, our bodies too creaky. Had we waited too long? We each underwent a battery of tests—and speaking only for myself, let me just say I hope never to see a plastic specimen jar again—and eventually found out we were fine. It was just that our margin of error had shrunk. If we were going to start a family without any outside help, it would be only as a best-case scenario. We had a chance, but it was more worst-to-first in 1991 than it was defending World Series champs in 1996. Getting pregnant was emotionally draining, but I tried to think of it as a marathon instead of a sprint, tried to keep my hopes high, to believe in yes rather than no.

For the first half of 2010, the Braves were my great distraction. Despite Heyward's nuclear start, the Braves finished April with more losses than wins, mostly because nobody else seemed to be able to get a hit. In May, everyone started hitting at once and they caught fire, going 20–8 for the month, and on Memorial Day they passed the Phillies to move into first place in the National League East for the first time since 2005. They sustained it throughout June and July, and entered August with a robust record of 59–46.

On the afternoon of August 3, I was sitting at my desk at work at *SLAM,* trying to think up some creative way we could photograph LeBron James as a new member of the Miami Heat for our next cover story. That evening, the Braves were hosting the Mets. The Braves had been sitting on a healthy five- or six-game lead over Philadelphia, but it had atrophied down to three games. Now the Phils were breathing down our necks, closing the gap. The pennant race was about to shift into high gear, and I was steeling myself for two months of living and dying with every pitch.

My phone rang.

"Hello?"

Before she even spoke, I knew it was my wife by this strange rattling sound on the other end of the line; I guess she has a flawed receiver on her work phone, and it always makes this almost imperceptible rattling noise. So I knew it was her. But that didn't temper the surprise of the words she spoke:

"I'm pregnant."

I felt my breath rush out of my body, and just as quickly it returned. We'd been seeing a reproductive doctor a couple of times each month since January, and Isabel had been taking drugs to induce ovulation, though it hadn't worked. We'd asked the doctor to give us July off, so we could travel, relax, and enjoy life, with the intention of returning in August and beginning in vitro fertilization. We'd spent some time in New England with my mom and dad, and spent a week out in Montana among the trees and rivers, and we'd come back recharged and ready to attack this pregnancy process with renewed vigor. And I should note, it was definitely a process. Having a child would be an ultimate joy and responsibility for us, but the constant doctor visits and tracking of cycles and taking pills and injections were mostly serving as a relentless reminder of the clinical, medical reality and improbability of what we were trying to accomplish.

Earlier in the day, Isabel had gone by the doctor's office for a simple blood test to make sure she was healthy enough to start the process of IVF. And whaddya know . . . she was knocked up.

I came home that night and settled in to watch the Braves and Mets, because watching the Braves is what I do. Everything that could have gone wrong did. After a tough April, Troy Glaus had been unbelievable in May and June, racking up a dozen home runs. Then he fell off some sort of cliff, turning in a thirty-five-game streak with no home runs and an average of .162, yet Bobby stuck with him. On this night, Bobby pulled

Glaus from the starting lineup, instead using reserve infielder Eric Hinske. (We would later learn Glaus had been battling a knee injury.) Derek Lowe started and pitched effectively, but Bobby pulled him and the bullpen struggled. In the eighth, with the game tied 2–2 and the bases loaded, Bobby selected Glaus to pinch hit against former Braves reliever Manny Acosta, and Glaus promptly grounded into a soul-crushing, inning-ending double play. In the top of the ninth, Bobby brought in Wagner, and he gave up a go-ahead home run to Jeff Francoeur. The Braves had won just the day before, but this loss felt like a slap in the face. We lost, lost late, at home, and even more horribly, it was at the hands of Acosta and Frenchy, two former Braves. I felt sick to my stomach. I should have been thrilled, considering the news I'd received earlier in the day, but this was crushing me. After the game I went on MLB.com and saw Cox's take on the loss: "We just need to score a few more runs. Everything is going great. Pitching has been going great. Defense, everything." The man just wasn't going to allow himself to get down about it. I resolved to stay positive as well.

Two days later we went to the fertility doctor, and after a quick exam, he spoke in a cautionary tone. While Isabel was indeed pregnant, it was still very early, and our age and history of having trouble getting pregnant weren't working in our favor. "I'd say the odds this takes are about fifty-fifty," the doctor said. Isabel and I walked out into the boiling New York City afternoon with our fingers entwined, tears of hope welling in our eyes, holding on to each other for dear life. Positivity, persistence, faith, patience: all these tenets ricocheted around my brain.

That night the Braves lost to the San Francisco Giants, and

that formerly healthy lead was now whittled down to one game. One freaking game. I needed this right now like I needed a hole in my head. Talk about stress, one day I blinked and unexpectedly I was neck deep in two races, one for a pennant, one for a pregnancy. It was going to take all the Bobby I could muster to make it through both.

The day that single-game Braves tickets for the 2010 season went on sale, I bought four seats for the Braves-Phillies game on Sunday, October 3. This would be the Braves' last home game of the season and, if the Braves didn't make the postseason, it had a chance of being Bobby Cox's final game as manager of the Braves.

As September rolled along, the Braves stumbled toward the finish. Heyward battled a few minor injuries but had a great season, finishing as a contender for Rookie of the Year. Yet after Chipper Jones went down, the Braves also lost Martin Prado, Jair Jurrjens, Kris Medlen, Takashi Saito, and Eric O'Flaherty to various injuries. As a result, they went 13–15 in September, which meant they slipped out of first place in the National League East but somehow stayed in first place in the wild card standings. I booked my flight to Atlanta for the final game of the season, hoping I could be there to cheer Bobby and the Braves on as they tried to sneak into the playoffs.

On Friday, October 1, two days before the MLB season ended and two days before I was set to fly to Atlanta to try to will the Braves into the playoffs, we hit the twelve-week mark of the pregnancy, and we went to the hospital for some routine tests. Isabel had spent most of the previous three months nauseous, and I'd spent most of that time nervous. We'd made it this far. Could we make it all the way to nine months?

At the hospital, after a few tests, the doctor on duty that morning set aside the sonogram wand and somberly turned to Isabel and me, then quietly told us that our baby had not made it. He apologized, as Isabel broke down in tears. I immediately forced my heaving emotions down into my gut and managed to stay detached, upbeat even, because I figured one of us needed to be levelheaded to deal with whatever was going to happen next. We went through a quick series of meetings with specialists and doctors, then left and went a few blocks over to see our ob-gyn.

Just outside the hospital, still in shock, the first call I made was to my mother, who was waiting to hear the results from the doctor's appointment. After managing to squeak out the news, I broke down crying. Before explaining the details, I had to ask my mom to wait a second, until I could catch my breath, calm my soul. I told her I wasn't going to be coming home that weekend. The chair beneath us that was precariously balanced on one leg suddenly had the final leg kicked out from under it.

My mom came to New York and nurtured us for the next week, like she's so good at doing. Instead of being in the stands at Turner Field, I ended up spending that Sunday on the couch, watching the Braves hang on and barely beat the Phillies to clinch a trip to the postseason. The Braves were in the playoffs, and although I knew this meant anything could happen, even a World Series win, I suspected it wouldn't, not with the way the Braves had been playing the last few weeks, not with so many important members of the team felled by injury.

I should have been excited, thrilled to see my team have

a chance at winning it all. In the days that followed, sadness found me in the most random places: on the subway, in the grocery store, on the couch late at night. Why couldn't I be a father? Why wasn't my wife allowed to be a mother? I tried to move on, but I felt like I couldn't escape. Isabel and I would sit in a restaurant and the couple next to us would talk about their kids, as I awkwardly tried to change the subject to current events or work. A commercial would come on TV featuring a mother and her newborn baby, and I'd silently flip the channel.

The Braves opened the National League playoffs against the San Francisco Giants. They lost game one in San Francisco after Giants starter Tim Lincecum came out and threw a brilliant two-hitter. One night later, Bobby got ejected in the second inning, and the Braves came from behind to push the game into extra innings. In the top of the eleventh, as the Braves prepared to send the bottom third of their lineup to the plate, I confidently explained to Isabel that the Braves weren't likely to score in that inning. Almost immediately, Rick Ankiel blasted a home run into McCovey Cove, putting the Braves on top for good and evening the series at 1–1. Suddenly, with the series shifting back to the familiar confines of Turner Field, it felt like the Braves really had a chance at knocking off the Giants.

Forty-eight hours later, back in Atlanta, the Braves and Giants tangled for game three. The Braves trailed all night, until our pinch-hitting specialist Eric Hinske came up in the bottom of the eighth and blasted a two-run homer to put the Braves ahead 2–1. Our closer, Billy Wagner, had been hurt in game two, so Bobby tried to mix and match bullpen matchups in the ninth to close out the game. The Braves were a strike away from taking a 2–1 series lead when the Giants rallied to tie the game. Then Brooks Conrad, the backup backup second baseman, committed his third error of the game, allowing the Giants to score the eventual game-winning run.

One night later, with the Braves on the brink of elimination, the Braves led for most of the game, until the Giants pulled ahead 3–2 in the seventh inning. The Braves got a man to second base in the eighth inning, and got two men on base in the ninth inning, but they just didn't have any magic left. The Giants won game four, 3–2, and when they recorded the third out in the ninth inning, the Giants players dutifully charged out onto the Turner Field infield to begin celebrating. The Giants were moving on; the Braves were finished. It wasn't much of a surprise, but it felt like the Braves just hadn't been able to get a break the entire series, seemingly getting bad bounces and calls against them every game. Every game in the series was decided by one run; the Braves just didn't win enough of them.

Most relevant, all of a sudden, Bobby Cox's career was over.

As the Giants players poured onto the field, the television cameras quickly cut to a shot of Cox in the Braves dugout, and he immediately disappeared into the tunnel behind the dugout. I wondered if that would be it, if this would be the last time we would ever see him in the Braves dugout.

While the Giants celebrated, the Atlanta fans started chanting "Bob-by, Bob-by!" Seconds later, Bobby reappeared. He ambled a few steps out of the Braves dugout and onto the dirt, then waved to the crowd, took off his cap, and held it up to the crowd. The noise swelled as the fans emoted their thanks. The Giants players, who seconds earlier had all been hopping around rejoicing, all stopped, turned to Cox, and applauded. ("He's the best manager for me that's ever managed the game," Giants outfielder Cody Ross would say later.) Cox pointed his left index finger toward Giants manager Bruce Bochy, acknowledging a series well played, and stood awkwardly for a few seconds in front of the dugout, surrounded by photographers. Then, for a final time, Bobby Cox walked back down the dugout stairs and disappeared into the clubhouse.

Cox next addressed the team in something of a postmortem meeting in the locker room. Chipper Jones said it was the only time in two decades he'd seen Bobby cry. "There wasn't a dry eye in the place," Chipper told the *AJC*. "I don't think I've cried in uniform since I was about eight. You spend as much time with Bobby as I have, it's hard. He's been a father figure to me; he's been my only manager. It's hard to swallow that this is going to be the last time."

The final time we fans saw Bobby in a Braves uniform was when Bobby held his postgame press conference. "I told them I was really proud of them, and um . . ." Cox leaned back from the microphone, crossed his arms, and put his left hand over his mouth. His eyebrows clinched together as he tried to fight back tears. Bobby stayed silent for eleven full seconds, trying to compose himself, before he grinned and said, "A grown man shouldn't do this."

It was unclear what the "this" was, but I assume he meant the tears. For me, sitting there alone on my couch in the dark, it all came loose. I'd spent two weeks trying to put on a brave public face while trying to figure out how to piece my world back together. And now it was hitting me that Bobby Cox, the constant in my life over the last two decades, was not going to be there any longer, either. Twenty-five years, a World Series win, fourteen consecutive division titles, 2,504 wins, fifteen seasons with at least 90 wins, countless hours spent sitting side by side in my imaginary dugout. Gone.

Considering everything I'd been going through, it actually felt pretty good to spend the next hour crying.

Two days after the season ended, the Braves held a press conference to announce that Fredi Gonzalez would be Bobby Cox's replacement. Gonzalez had spent five years coaching in the Braves organization in the early 2000s before managing the Florida Marlins for three and a half seasons. Announcing his return to Atlanta, Gonzalez took a seat alongside Bobby at a press conference. Bobby was wearing a sports coat and dress shirt, Gonzalez a Braves jersey and cap. Bobby talked about his future. "I really don't want to be too organized anymore on a time schedule. I've been that way for a long time, half a century."

Speaking about Gonzalez, Bobby said, "About replacing me, that's crazy. You know Walter Alston was replaced by Tommy Lasorda, who was a scout and then a minor league manager. He did a great job and they forgot all about Walter Alston. That's what's going to happen here."

As terrific as it would be if Fredi Gonzalez has a run with the Braves as successful as Tommy Lasorda had after replacing Walter Alston with the Dodgers—1,599 wins, two World Series championships—nobody will forget about Bobby Cox, at least no Braves fans who have had any casual interest in the team in the last two decades. I'm not sure if I'll connect with Fredi the way I did with Bobby, but I'm willing to give it a shot.

Bobby Cox may be my favorite sports manager of all time, but the Braves are my favorite team, and I know pretty much anyone who puts on an Atlanta Braves uniform has my heart. They at least get the benefit of the doubt.

My hope was to be able to end this book with the Braves sending Bobby Cox off with an improbable world championship, and my wife and I finally on our way to starting a family. Instead, you've read the way things worked out, or rather, didn't work out. Now the Braves were moving on, Bobby was moving on. And I knew I needed to move on as well.

It took me a few days, but what I eventually had to accept was that no matter how much I care, no matter how hard I try, I can't control the future. What I can affect is how I approach each day.

Reaching the point in my life where I am today has been a wild and unpredictable ride, and the last few weeks of the 2010 season were some of the toughest weeks of my life. But me, I'm choosing to look forward with hope. Perhaps things won't always shake out the way I'm hoping they will. But I will let go of the things I have no control over, work as hard as I can, give my best effort. I don't know what the future holds, for me or for the Braves. But I have twenty years of lessons from which to draw, and no matter what life throws at me, be it a two-seam fastball at my hands or a hanging slider right down Peachtree, I have decided that I will move forward, forward, forward.

And I'm hoping for the best.

ACKNOWLEDGMENTS

If you made it this far, thank you. Writing this book has been the hardest thing I've ever done in my life. I went to work every day, came home and had dinner with my wife, waited for her to go to sleep, and then stayed up until 2:00 a.m. every night to write. Then I woke up early the next morning to start the whole thing all over again.

Enormous thanks to my literary agent, Alison Schwartz at ICM. Thank you for four years of calls, emails, texts, dinners, and an international vacation, but mostly friendship. I cannot thank you enough, Ali.

Thank you to my family at *SLAM* for being understanding throughout this process—Dennis, Ben, Susan, Melissa, Ryne, Tzvi, Matt, Ramon, Adam, Schnur, and the MVP, Spiro. Thanks also to the Antenna crew, including Kaity and Sarah.

Thanks to my writing mentors and advisers and friends, including Russ Bengtson, Nathaniel Friedman, Tony Gervino, Ryan Jones, Alan Paul, Sam Rubenstein, Mike Sager, Khalid

Salaam, Datwon Thomas, Bonsu Thompson, Elliott Wilson, and Dave Zirin.

Thanks to my ATL guys: Al, Dave, Matt, Mike, Steve, Todd, and Bruce.

Thanks to the Atlanta Braves and Adam Liberman. Also, thanks to Kate Hart at SportSouth for research materials. And my friend Todd for loaning me his Braves DVD vault.

Thanks to my family: Mom and Dad, Claire and Andrew, Liza and Megan.

In closing, you would not be reading this without the tireless work of my editor at Scribner, Brant Rumble. Even though he went to some fancy Midwestern college, Brant is at heart a Southern man, and, most important, a Braves fan, which saved both of us a lot of time looking up stats and names and instances. Thanks also to Anna DeVries and Kathleen Rizzo at Scribner. I know that all of you worked to make this project the best it could be.

And finally, thanks to Isabel. I realize that I will never be able to thank you enough. I love you with all of my heart. We've been through a lot together, and thank you for allowing me the leeway to share our journey with the world. I'm eternally thrilled to have you by my side, and I'm proud every day to be by your side.

Oh, and to Bobby Cox: Thank you for being you. And even though you didn't know you were doing it, thank you for making me, me.

One last thing: Go Braves.